D0929906

"In our world, we like to 'get things done' but seldom take time to mold the leaders of tomorrow. Preston Poore's new book combines spiritual insight with the nuts and bolts of solid leadership. In *Discipled Leader*, Preston offers readers practical guidance on how to apply timeless Christian principles to leadership. It's a must-read for every leader."

DAN T. CATHY, chairman and CEO of Chick-fil-A, Inc.

"You have the potential to be a difference-maker in today's chaotic, leadership-starved world. But to see positive change in others, you must first allow yourself to be changed. In *Discipled Leader*, Preston Poore connects a Christian leader's need for personal discipleship to their leadership calling. This inspiring and practical book, written by a man who's been in the trenches of both life and leadership, will guide you toward better leadership by way of better discipleship."

CHRIS ROBINSON, executive vice president of The John Maxwell Team

"Preston Poore has learned through life experience that leadership truly flows from who we are, not from what we do. In *Discipled Leader*, Preston provides the rationale and tools to help leaders develop a strong, Christ-centered foundation for unimpeachable character and lasting influence."

ANGIE WARD, assistant director of the doctor of ministry program at Denver Seminary

"Preston's years of wisdom, gained from integrating and living out his faith in the workplace, are displayed in *Discipled Leader*. Leaders will be challenged and encouraged to bring their whole selves to the workplace as they learn from the practical experiences Preston shares."

DAVE KATZ, president and COO of Coca-Cola Consolidated, Inc.

"Preston Poore has written the field manual for anyone who aspires to be an effective, impactful leader. *Discipled Leader* makes a clear and persuasive case for development through discipleship. Future difference-makers who apply these biblical principles will see powerful results!"

JOHN FEATHERSTON, senior director of new ventures at Chick-fil-A, Inc.

"Experience is the most powerful teacher, and today's Christian leaders must quickly grow from all experiences—both good and bad. Through inspiring stories and wisdom, Preston Poore gives guidance to Christians who can learn from his life and career challenges. Odds are you will find counsel for your own situation in *Discipled Leader*."

DEAN CROWE, founder and CEO of Rally Foundation for Childhood Cancer Research

"*Discipled Leader* provides practical tools, tips, and action points for living out the basic Christian disciplines. Preston's personal stories are moving and lead the reader to see how applying these principles makes a difference. This resource is useful for new believers or someone who has followed Christ for years. It encourages and equips the individual but can also be used as a group study with the discussion questions and facilitator guide. *Discipled Leader* is a great resource for anyone desiring to walk closer with the Lord."

BRYANT WRIGHT, president of Send Relief, former senior pastor at Johnson Ferry Baptist Church, and founder of Right from the Heart Ministries

"I recommend this book for those who desire to take their relationship with God to the next level. *Discipled Leader* provides a good balance between teaching principles and practical application. The personal stories are powerful in connecting the principles to real life and compelling you to action. Preston does a wonderful job of appealing to both the head and the heart, which is key to growth. Buckle up and get ready to be transformed."

DAWN S. KIRK, owner of Kirk Coaching Group, author of *Heartbeat Leadership*, best-selling coauthor of *The Success Blueprint*, entrepreneur, speaker, and former Fortune 100 executive

"Whatever leadership is, it isn't easy. Business leaders face the daily challenges of ambiguity, uncertainty, risk, conflict, and much more. In *Discipled Leader*, Preston Poore shows how Christian values and beliefs can guide leaders to do the right things, which in secular commerce may be called governance, stewardship, equality, engagement, and empowerment. In truth, these are all entirely congruent with the Christian faith, and being a discipled leader ensures unparalleled and infectious strength, faith, and courage. The undeniable connection between discipleship and effective leadership in modern-day business is beautifully highlighted in this must-read book."

STEPHEN GIBSON, managing director and chartered business psychologist at Gibson Hallmark Ltd.

"There is no command to make converts in Scripture! There is a command to make disciples. However, that command is ignored, watered down, redefined, and disobeyed. Preston Poore not only lays out the biblical mandate in a very real manner but also makes it practical. I especially like that *Discipled Leader* is geared for small groups where encouragement and accountability can and should exist. Read this book and join in the excitement of becoming like Jesus. Pass it forward."

DR. HAL HADDEN, founder of Christian Leadership Concepts

"*Discipled Leader* offers spiritual and practical tools to lead exceptionally with prayer, peace, perseverance, and promise. As leaders, it can be difficult to see how your faith and leadership interact, but this book helps readers understand effective ways to lead with power."

ALLISON LIDDLE, best-selling author, leadership trainer at Allison Liddle Consulting, president of Prosper Wealth Management, and participant on *The Social Movement* TV series

"A serious book for people seriously wanting to become, and help others become, disciples! And if you're not serious about wanting to be a discipled and discipling leader, about what are you serious? *Discipled Leader* is a well-executed effort to help believers be strong in the Lord and help others do the same. An unashamed mix of solid theology, intentional action, and strict accountability, this is a book to put into practice! I pray that God will use *Discipled Leader* to produce just that—leaders who are disciples making disciples."

DR. BOB EWELL, church discipleship consultant with The Navigators

"Powerful, insightful, foundational, practical, life-altering, timely, and a must-read! Preston has written a work that is not just another book but a tool that can help any sincere individual empower their faith to go from head knowledge to heart knowledge and then to practical life knowledge. Our culture is not in desperate need of more knowledge but of more application that results in real-life transformation! Maybe like no other time in American history, Christianity is at a crossroads of conviction and faith. Tools like what Preston has developed are essential for such a time as this. Having known Preston for almost forty years, I can attest that this book is not simply what he wrote but something he lives. Do yourself a favor and immerse yourself in this work."

JEFF CRABTREE, lead pastor, founder, and president of Connections Church, and founder and president of Life Connections Network and Next Level Life Coaching

"Preston Poore has written a masterpiece. *Discipled Leader* is a must-read for anyone focused on moving their life's work from 'ordinary' to 'extraordinary' in the area of spiritual leadership. The book serves as a dynamic balance for positive action for Christians who truly want to make a difference, change their world, and lead with joy."

IRA BLUMENTHAL, founder and president of CO-OPPORTUNITIES, Inc., and best-selling author of *Managing Brand You*

"Jesus equipped his disciples for a singular task and a simple strategy: make disciples who make disciples. *Discipled Leader* builds a bridge between Jesus's training of his first-century followers and the day-to-day lives of twenty-first-century believers. Those who humbly traverse this bridge will find themselves informed, transformed, and re-formed as Jesus's disciples. My advice: Learn from the content but don't fail to listen prayerfully to the heart. If you listen, you will hear the voice of a Savior reaching through you into the world."

RICK DUNN, lead pastor of Fellowship Church, coauthor of *Shaping the Journey of Emerging Adults*, and author of *The Northfield Way*

DISCIPLED LEADER

DISCIPLED LEADER

Inspiration from a Fortune 500 Executive for Transforming Your Workplace by Pursuing Christ

Preston Poore

KREGEL
PUBLICATIONS

Discipled Leader: Inspiration from a Fortune 500 Executive for Transforming Your Workplace by Pursuing Christ
© 2021 by Preston Poore

Published by Kregel Publications, a division of Kregel Inc., 2450 Oak Industrial Dr. NE, Grand Rapids, MI 49505.

Persons and events portrayed in this book have been used with permission. To protect the privacy of individuals, some names and identifying details have been changed.

Cataloging-in-Publication Data is on file with the Library of Congress.

ISBN 978-0-8254-4693-1, print
ISBN 978-0-8254-7741-6, epub

Printed in the United States of America
21 22 23 24 25 26 27 28 29 30 / 5 4 3 2 1

To my beautiful bride,
Carla,
who has always believed in me and this project.

To our children and legacy,
Caroline and Benton,
for whom we are so grateful.

CONTENTS

FOREWORD

MY FIRST MEANINGFUL leadership discussion with Preston Poore occurred on the patio of a small diner on the campus of the University of Tennessee. Like true Southerners, we talked faith, family, and football over plates of fried chicken and ice-cold Coca-Colas.

The conversation naturally turned toward our shared passion for leading well. Preston offered, "I want to tell you my story." With that simple, humble introduction, he invited me further into his life. In doing so, he also invited me to journey further into the life of Jesus.

Long after we had consumed our Southern cuisine, Preston and I eagerly explored the practical realities of Jesus's singular missional command: make disciples. The longer we talked, the more substantially two very specific desires planted their roots deep within me. First, I longed to understand more about how gifted leaders can take daily, practical steps toward becoming discipled leaders. Second, I wanted to learn, not only from Preston but with him, how to take those steps in my own life.

Discipled Leader stirred those desires once again. I am confident it will do the same for you. By telling his story, Preston offers both himself and his Savior to the reader. As he pairs his story with key discipleship principles in the Scriptures, Preston unveils Jesus's powerful vision for our leadership journeys. To personalize that vision, he provides critical reflection questions that guide us on a practical path forward.

On the one hand, this book cannot quite reproduce the personal intimacy of the conversation Preston and I had on that patio years ago. However, if you read *Discipled Leader* prayerfully, with or without fried chicken and a Coke, I am confident you will come very close to that moment. I am also convinced that you, like Preston, will soon find yourself sitting across the table from a friend or colleague, offering your own story as a pathway to Jesus. That's just what discipled leaders do.

And it's precisely how God changes the world, more simply and more profoundly than we could ever have imagined, one discipled leader at a time.

"Now to him who is able to do immeasurably more than all we ask or imagine, according to his power that is at work within us, to him be glory in the church and in Christ Jesus throughout all generations, for ever and ever! Amen" (Eph. 3:20–21 NIV).

Entrusted by Grace,
Rick Dunn, PhD
Fellowship Church, Lead Pastor

ACKNOWLEDGMENTS

I WROTE *DISCIPLED Leader* over the course of ten years and have many to thank for their help along the way.

My family: To Carla, my beautiful and incredible wife, for patiently enduring with me along this journey. One spring evening in 1993, I shared my dream of writing a book while we were on a walk in Homewood, Alabama. You've been with me all the way, and I appreciate your continuing support.

To Caroline and Benton, my blessings: I am so proud of you and who you are becoming!

To Mom and Dad, thank you for modeling love, commitment, and hard work. Your example helped me believe that we can make dreams come true.

To Jeff and Emily, thank you for your life partnership and entrepreneurial spirit.

To Carlton and Camilla, thank you for adopting me into your family and being great role models. I love all of you!

My agent: To Steve Hutson and WordWise Media. Thank you for taking a chance on me. I'll always remember eating lunch with you in Los Angeles's iconic Original Pantry Café and talking about what's possible.

My publisher: To Catherine DeVries, Steve Barclift, Katherine Chappell, and the team at Kregel Publications. Thank you for partnering with me to expand *Discipled Leader*'s reach.

My editors: To Joel Armstrong, Blake Atwood, and Mike Towel. Joel, thank you for helping my message reach its full potential. Blake, thank you for helping me find my voice. Mike, thank you for helping to structure my thoughts.

My mentors: To Rick Dunn, Bob Ewell, David Bianconi, and Jeff Crabtree. I stand on your shoulders and appreciate the examples you've been to me over the years.

My Atlanta Christian Leadership Concepts (CLC) group: To Tom Bradley, Shawn Brasfield, Kevin Chalk, Jerry Chang, Bruce Denning, Mark Durden, Walter Fleming, Bob Holz, Rick Manzo, Chris McKemie, Russ Mullins, and Brad Smith. You guys are awesome and have inspired me in so many ways!

My initial Discipled Leader *training participants at Johnson Ferry Baptist Church*: To Michelle Cavelier, Rebecca Daniel, Sam Fernandes, Sharyn Godley, Richard Jones, Judith McCoy, Carla Poore, Paula Kimick, Rob Milam, Catherine Milam, Jodie Cox, Katie Cox, Pillar Garcia, and Wes Fincher. Thanks to all of you for taking a chance and sharing your stories. I saw growth in each one of you!

To those in my career who modeled the way and inspired me to become a better leader, including Rick Kehr, Ron Renner, Michael Mathews, Jim Lactaoen, and John Egan. Thank you for believing in me, putting me in positions to grow, and bringing out the best in me.

To countless others, including Buddy Pelot, Drew Meadows, Edwin Gotay, Gary Adams, John Featherston, Hal Hadden, Ashley Saunders, Lynn Pinyerd, Tim Leveridge, Mark Spence, Eric Brewton, Tom and Chris Ronchetti, Kevin Whitehead, Ken Mied, Annette Harlow, and Paul Beersdorf. I truly appreciate your feedback and editing during the writing process.

Where Are Today's Christian Leaders?

Everybody thinks of changing humanity,
and nobody thinks of changing himself.
—LEO TOLSTOY, "THREE METHODS OF REFORM"

SHORTLY AFTER I was promoted to a management position in 2005, I had two direct reports quit within six months of each other. I will never forget their similar reasons for leaving, which they made sure to tell me: "I just don't like the way you treat me, Preston. And, well, you're condescending."

Me? Condescending? I thought. *As if they know the pressure I have to deal with. Like they have the experience to do what I do.*

Before their departures, I thought I was on the fast track to success. I figured that if I continued driving change, performing well, and delivering results during my new assignment, I would be promoted again. My leadership skills were blooming, and I was confident in my ability to make a positive difference.

But somewhere in my ambition to succeed, I lost my focus on God.

I started leaving him at home and did not live out my Christian faith in the workplace. I saw my faith and work as two separate things. My priorities got out of whack; my thoughts and actions were self-serving. I didn't necessarily care about people, only what they could do for me.

All too soon, our results nose-dived. I struggled to gain traction with my new manager, team, and business partners. I constantly bickered with my manager and always felt like I had to prove myself. I felt mal-treated and disrespected.

I saw my team as a means to an end and never made any true connec-tions. Then those two direct reports left. Covering for my lost employ-ees, I constantly traveled and consequently exhausted myself.

Careerwise, I had hit rock bottom. At that point, I journaled:

> My heart is heavy today. I feel crushed. The past few weeks were extremely difficult. Another employee quit, I received feedback on my condescending tone again, role shift, and an overall feel-ing of devaluation. My manager continues to dissect every com-ment I make and criticize my actions. This year's been a valley of despair. I feel torn apart and weak.

Inevitably, my challenges at work spilled over to my home life, where I was always irritable. To top it off, my beloved grandfather, Papa, passed away.

Something had to change.

Thankfully, my manager directed me to engage an executive coach to help me fix things. And so I did. I also began to pray and read the Bible more intentionally. I sought God's help in the depths of my despair. As I prayed and worked with my coach, I realized the common thread in all my issues was *me*.

I was not acting like a leader—at my job, in my home, or of myself. My spiritual life and work life were incongruent. I went to church on Sunday but acted like an atheist during the workweek. At work, I thought I had all the leadership and management stuff figured out and did not need God's wisdom, help, or direction.

In other words, I was condescending even toward God.

Still, through these trials and tribulations, God answered my prayer and broke me. In my breaking, I realized I needed to change before I could create positive change in the workplace. I discovered that the surest way to realize my leadership potential was to become a follower of Jesus—not just on Sunday or at home but twenty-four hours a day, seven days a week. I needed to take what I learned in the church pew and live it out in the workplace.

I needed to become a discipled leader.

I have worked at Fortune 500 companies for decades. I know what it is like to be responsible for multimillion-dollar budgets, to lead employees of all kinds, and to work for highly driven executives. I have been blessed to be recognized within my industry many times over for the work that my team and I have accomplished. I believe I am a hard worker who asks the best of myself and my employees. My professional path has not always been smooth—whose is? But I remain grateful for every job I have had. My career has given me much.

But I never want to lose sight of my first calling as a disciple of Christ.

Yet, when you spend forty to eighty hours a week at your job, it is easy to lose perspective. You slide into the false belief that what you do defines who you are rather than allowing who you are to define what you do. And if you are a Christian, who you are is a disciple of Christ.

By *disciple* I mean someone who passionately pursues an intimate fellowship with Jesus, seeking his presence, will, wisdom, and guidance in every facet of life—family, work, school, and community. In collaboration with the Holy Spirit, disciples are intentionally growing in their faith through consistent practices like Bible study, prayer, and fellowship with other believers. As disciples develop Christlike character, their changed lives can't help but change the world around them. God works in them and through them to accomplish his purposes as the disciples actively participate in God's work.

So why does it seem like there is a dearth of disciples in today's secular marketplace? Why does it sometimes feel as if you're the only Christian at your workplace? How are you supposed to bring the world-opposing tenets of the Christian faith to bear on your everyday professional decisions?

Who you are must change before what you do changes.

Honestly—and it took me a long time to figure this out—it is not about changing your leadership style. While learning how to be a better leader is necessary, and many excellent books have been written to that end, changing your style will not change who you are.

Who you are must change before what you do changes.

In the following chapters, I will share personal stories that delve into the seldom-discussed connection between personal discipleship and corporate leadership. Each story is accompanied by two imperatives: one for your spiritual life and one for your leadership. I hope you will see how these imperatives are connected to each other within each chapter. I pray that you will begin to notice and experience how what you hear from God in the quiet of your morning prayers translates to effective leadership, even in the noise of a busy workday.

If you are a struggling Christian leader in the secular marketplace, I pray you will be challenged to engage in the hard work of daily discipleship. If you are an experienced leader, I pray you will be reminded of the fundamentals of the faith and the desperate need to disciple other Christian leaders.

Becoming who you are meant to be as a Christian leader does not begin with focusing on *leadership*. Your calling toward better leadership is a calling toward deeper *discipleship*.

That's how you become a discipled leader.

HOW TO GET THE MOST OUT OF THIS BOOK

Set your intention and remain intentional. Why did you decide to invest time reading this book? What do you hope to gain regarding discipleship and leadership? Understand the why and what, and then be intentional to achieve them.

Focus on the anchor Scripture. Each chapter starts with a key verse. Take time to read it and the surrounding context in your Bible.

Pause and reflect. It is easy to read and not think about what you have read. Pause while you are engaged in the material, then reflect on what it means and how you would apply the principles. Consider highlighting, marking, and writing notes in the margins.

Answer and discuss the study questions. Review and think deeply about your answers. Compare your thoughts with the material and with other people's responses.

Apply, apply, apply. You learn by doing. Apply each priniciple to your everyday life, otherwise the material will go in one ear and out the other.

Take notes on what you've learned. After applying a principle, write down what you experienced and learned. Did you succeed or fail? What will you do next time?

Share your story. Once you have read, applied, and learned, share your story with someone else. Sharing your story will help you to teach others or will enable them to hold you accountable to living out the principles in this book.

CHAPTER ONE

SEEK

As a disciple, invest time with God.

As a leader, seek God when making decisions.

Every Scripture is God-breathed (given by His inspiration)
and profitable for instruction, for reproof and conviction of sin,
for correction of error and discipline in obedience, [and] for
training in righteousness (in holy living, in conformity to God's
will in thought, purpose, and action), so that the man of God
may be complete and proficient, well fitted and thoroughly
equipped for every good work.

—2 TIMOTHY 3:16–17 AMPC

My wife, Carla, sat silently in the passenger seat. We had just left dinner with some new professional acquaintances, and I thought the opportunities that had been presented to us looked very promising. I was lost in a whirlwind of hopeful thinking when Carla's voice broke into my future plans.

"Preston, something doesn't feel right about Hunter and his wife. Everything sounds great, but I don't think the role is the right thing for you or us. I don't want you to take the job."

I could not believe my wife's words. Why couldn't she see the incredible opportunity Hunter was offering us? I was so frustrated. We drove the rest of the way home in silence.

A few months earlier, I was a struggling salesman. I could not close accounts or secure large orders. I did not understand how to open a sales call, handle objections, or present benefits over features. So I enrolled in a local sales-training course.

That's when I met Hunter.

He owned the training franchise and was my instructor. I instantly connected with him. He was a charismatic leader and a successful salesperson, and he was out to make a positive difference. And he backed it up with an impressive résumé. He was the number-one salesperson for his international training organization two years in a row. He conducted training with many Fortune 500 companies, played on the PGA tour, and even hosted a local radio program. Hunter's success enabled him to live in a luxurious house, enjoy a country club membership, and drive a sports car. Hunter seemed to have it all.

I wanted to be like Hunter.

He was also a gifted facilitator, and I was inspired by his selling principles. With Hunter's help, I grew personally and professionally as the class progressed. In fact, I ended up winning the class sales-talk competition. As I got to know Hunter, I learned about his mission to develop people and help them reach their potential. Hunter's mission spoke to my heart, his lifestyle appealed to my ego, and his work was in line with what I had dreamed of doing someday.

I wanted to change careers and achieve the same success. I believed if I attached myself to Hunter and his mission, I would move into a job with greater significance. So I told Hunter I wanted to work with him and transition careers to the training industry.

He liked the idea and offered me a robust compensation package, including a base salary, commission, and a quarterly bonus. All I had to do was fill training courses and develop new business opportunities. To close the deal, Hunter and his wife invited us to dinner. They believed it was essential to meet Carla and gain her commitment to the role as well.

The restaurant was on the top floor of a downtown skyscraper overlooking the city skyline. As we enjoyed great food and wine, I thought, *I could get used to this.* Hunter and his wife explained the business, the role I would play, and why they wanted me to join their company. They made the opportunity sound amazing.

At that moment, I told myself I wanted the role for all the right reasons: to make a positive difference in people's lives, to exercise my talents and skills, and to engage the community. Nothing was going to deter me from the future that surely awaited us.

Over the next couple of days, my resolve deepened. I convinced Carla to come along. I promoted my agenda and said all the right things. Was I in God's Word? Yep. At least, my eyes were passing over the pages of Scripture most days. Did I pray about it? Sure. But mostly to tell God what *I* thought would be best in the situation. Did I seek God's wise counsel? No, but I requested his "blessing"—by which I meant success, recognition, and a better lifestyle.

The truth is, I never slowed down to listen to God or Carla.

I invested all kinds of time in prospecting and speaking to civic clubs to drum up business leads. Sales rarely materialized, and I discovered how hard it is to sell an intangible, thousand-dollar product. The workdays were extremely long, selling during the day and attending training sessions at night. I always felt like I was on the verge of closing some big deals, but my activities rarely led to accomplishment. I had a hard time making any commission or bonuses.

Then my personal Black Monday hit. I walked into my office one day and found a letter from Hunter in my mailbox. My salary and bonuses were cut. I had been moved to a draw plus commission. The different compensation package meant Hunter would loan money to me monthly, and I would pay him back through a percentage of my sales. If my commissions were over the draw, I would be rewarded with additional income. If not, I would owe Hunter money.

I had known the role would be tough, but that kind of compensation package was not what I signed up for. I pressed Hunter. He told me I could leave at any time. Then he began distancing himself from me and no longer offered support. I was isolated and scared.

The next six months were challenging for Carla and me. I often did not earn enough to make up the draw and so owed Hunter money. The lack of income and job anxiety put a lot of pressure on our marriage. I wondered why God ever let me get into the situation. Then it hit me.

And I felt like an idiot.

Signs and messages had been all around me not to take the job. In fact, God's most vocal sign had sat next to me in the immediate aftermath of the job offer. To my chagrin, I ignored her and the inner conflict deep in my soul that I was seeking worldly fulfillment and accomplishment rather than the abundant life God was calling me to. I had exercised terrible judgment, and the pain we experienced was self-inflicted.

I got on my knees and sought God's forgiveness for not listening to him. I began to ask how I could seek his will rather than mine. I asked for wisdom, discernment, and help to navigate the rough waters. I also asked Carla for forgiveness for not listening to her and choosing to advance my agenda. I had been so sure of myself, and I had not led us well. I had made a colossal mistake and admitted it to her in shame. Thankfully, she forgave me.

I accepted the consequences of my career decision and developed an exit strategy. I worked hard to break even with the draw. With God's help, I found a more stable job in another industry. Even though the situation was tough, God was glorified in the end, and he worked things out for my family's good.

But what an unfortunate and unnecessary detour!

SEEK WISDOM

Maybe my detour was not totally unnecessary. I did learn an invaluable truth about leadership: discipled leaders seek God when making decisions. And leaders have to make *a lot* of decisions.

Typically a leader's daily decision-making process includes defining the problem or opportunity, determining root causes, brainstorming potential solutions and implications, choosing the optimal solution, acting on the decision, and examining its impact. (We will explore how to make sound workplace decisions and solve challenging problems later in this chapter.) Decision-making ranges from simple to complex. The more facts, logic, analysis, advice, and experience, the better. But what happens when the circumstances are ambiguous and you do not have all the facts? Where do you turn in a crisis, or while dealing with challenging people, or in the midst of a rapidly changing environment?

Good decision makers often turn to intuition, that inner voice, sense, hunch, or gut feeling that arises when making a decision. Intuition is a feeling you have about the decision, good or bad. Leaders combine information, experience, and intuition to make hard decisions.

But let's be honest: our intuition is often wrong. The Bible says, "There is a way that seems right to a man, but its end is the way to death" (Prov. 14:12). Australian writer Christina Stead writes, "Intuition is not infallible; it only seems to be the truth."[1] If our intuition can be wrong, what is the disciplined leader to do?

The key to not just good but great decision-making is to seek God. A disciplined leader soaks in God's Word and asks for wisdom (James 1:5).

This is the surest way to seek God's guidance. A disciplined leader also recognizes other people (such as my wife) who are soaking themselves in God's Word and can speak wisdom into the leader's life. God is the source of wisdom, and he can see things you cannot. As the following sections explore, you can learn how to read God's Word to help you distinguish what is true and right. The Bible says, "Your word is a lamp to my feet and a light to my path" (Ps. 119:105). Regarding my opportunity with Hunter, had I honestly sought God and his wisdom instead of convincing myself that I knew what to do, I would have avoided the self-inflicted pain.

Perhaps this approach to decision-making both in and out of the workplace surprises you. The Bible is full of spiritual insight and moral teaching, you may think to yourself, but what does it have to do with making tough calls as a leader? Isn't it a little outdated for the business world? Before we consider how to read God's Word for wisdom in our lives as disciples and leaders, let's look at what the Word of God is and how it came to us.

THE WORD BROUGHT TO LIFE

What makes the Bible special, more useful and life changing than any book on leadership, psychology, or business management ever could be? In a daily quiet time book titled *The Experience*, Henry and Richard Blackaby write about the Bible's uniqueness:

> The difference between other books and God's Word is that the Bible is more than words on a page. It is alive and powerful. . . . When you need to make a change in your life, *the Holy Spirit will take the Scriptures and work them out in your life.* You can read your Bible with confidence that God has the power to do anything he wants in the lives of people.[2]

The Bible calls the Word of God "living and active, sharper than any two-edged sword, piercing to the division of soul and of spirit, of joints and of marrow, and discerning the thoughts and intentions of the heart" (Heb. 4:12), but to read the Bible for all it's worth and to experience spiritual growth, you must have a specific partner in prayer: the Holy Spirit. The Holy Spirit brings God's Word to life in our hearts. Once you trust Jesus and commit your life to him, he gives you a thirst for him and his Word. When you read the Bible, it shapes and forms your mind, beliefs, and behaviors. You are given the desire and motivation to obey the words of the Bible through the help of the Holy Spirit.

To some, the Holy Spirit is a nebulous part of the Trinity: an unknowable entity that hovers here and there and does something for us, but we are not sure what. But the Holy Spirit is much more than that and integral to the life of every believer. If you feel that you do not quite understand the role of the Holy Spirit in your life, it may help to think about a sailboat gliding on the water. What propels it? The sails capture the wind, and it moves the boat forward. In 2 Timothy 3, Paul writes that God "breathed" his Word, the Bible. The Greek word for *breathed* describes a ship with its wind-filled sails carried along the water.[3] Just like the wind with a sailboat, God blew wind into the sails of the Bible's authors, guiding and carrying them along.

What was this wind God blew? The Holy Spirit. Also in 2 Timothy 3, Paul says that *all Scripture* is the product of the Holy Spirit's work. The Holy Spirit filled the writers and propelled them so that the produced words—though they still bear the marks of the writers' personalities—remained the true and certain words of God himself.[4] In other words, God revealed his truth and thoughts to men and inspired them to record it.

Because the Holy Spirit *is* God, and he inspired the Bible, we must conclude that it is not a book manufactured by humans with good thoughts, sayings, or moral advice. God actively superintended its writing. When you read the Bible, God is speaking to *you*, and the Holy Spirit helps you understand what he is saying. What a wonderful gift!

Because the Bible is inspired, breathed, and originated by God, it can be trusted. It is a divine-human book. It is unique. It has no errors. It is the truth and wholly true. It is *the* standard for all moral dealings. It defines reality. It is relevant, reliable, and infallible. It is credible and authoritative. It reveals God's will. It is both spiritual and historical. It is transformative. It is living and active. It is worth dying for.

*Time alone with God is at the very heart
of the Christian walk.*

The message of the Bible is also unified. Every Scripture communicates God's love for us and his continual pursuit of us, despite our depravity. He loves us so much that he gave his only Son, Jesus, to redeem us from our bondage and restore our relationship with him. This is the central, unifying message of the Bible. All of Scripture points to Jesus as our Savior. He is the source of life and fills our lives with hope and joy. God not only inspired his Word, but he also influences, motivates, and stirs us through his Son, Jesus, whose life, death, and resurrection are the culmination of Scripture.

CONNECT DAILY

If God is going to mature, equip, and use you as a disciple of Christ and a leader in the workplace to have a ripple effect in the world, it is essential that you are in his Word daily, seeking his wisdom and listening to his voice. This simple act is commonly referred to as a "quiet time."

Time alone with God is at the very heart of the Christian walk. It is your appointment with God Almighty. It is more than a routine; it is about a relationship. God desires fellowship with you and wants you to get to know him better. A quiet time is an invitation to be with him, to hear him speak through his Word, to say you're sorry when you have wronged him, to be thankful, to lay your burdens at his feet, to gain wisdom, to renew your strength, and to receive hope. God loves you and wants to be near you. If you draw near to him, he will draw near to you (James 4:8).

Your challenge is that the devil does not want you to spend with God. The devil does not want you to be transformed so you can transform your culture. He will distract you and give you every excuse available not to meet with God, read the Bible, or pray. If you are like me, you will hear the excuse that you are too busy to make time to read the Bible. Or it is going to be boring and you will not get anything out of it anyway. Or it is too complicated and too many people have argued about it to know how to read it right. Even when you do have a quiet time, your enemy will throw everything at you to prevent you from applying what you have learned from God.

The devil will also cause you to doubt and ask, "Did God really say that?" Christian, be alert! If you struggle with your daily quiet time, you need to recognize that God is bigger than the devil. Ask for the Holy Spirit's help to give you the desire to have a quiet time. Ask for a thirst for God's Word, and seek him in prayer.

EIGHT GUIDING PRINCIPLES FOR QUIET TIMES

Along with the Holy Spirit's help, we also need to do our part to prioritize our quiet time and glean God's Word for wisdom. To ensure that I stay tuned in to God daily, I try to incorporate these eight principles for a productive and effective quiet time:

- *Place:* Find somewhere private without distractions. Do not allow your phone, TV, the internet, or any other thing to keep you from focusing on your time with God. My regular spot is sitting in our family room recliner because I can control the environment and I am able to concentrate.
- *Time:* I am a morning person and find that I am better able to concentrate at the start of the day. I have fewer troubles on my mind than at the end of the day. Consequently, I have more energy in the mornings. This might be the opposite for many. Choose a time that works best for you. Plan for ten to twenty minutes each day, and make your quiet time a priority.
- *Opening prayer:* This is the critical way to start your daily quiet time. I confess my sins and then ask the Holy Spirit to guide me and grant me wisdom as I read his Word.
- *Reading:* I typically use a daily devotional to guide my Scripture

selection (e.g., Oswald Chambers's *My Utmost for His Highest*). I read the context around the Scripture and then go to the commentary. It is important to be in the Bible and not use the devotional guide as "spiritual fast food." The true power is in the Bible, not the devotional or commentary. At other times, I read a chapter of Proverbs according to the date. For example, I read Proverbs 7 on June 7. Proverbs has thirty-one chapters, which works out to one chapter each day for a month. At other times I choose a book of the Bible and read a chapter per day. If you take this route, I recommend starting with the gospel of John.

- *Memorization:* Choose a few Scriptures that have special meaning to you and commit them to memory. This will allow you to recall them and think about them at any time.

- *Meditation:* J. I. Packer describes meditation as "an activity of holy thought, consciously performed in the presence of God, under the eye of God, by the help of God, as a means of communication with God. Its purpose is to clear one's mental and spiritual vision of God and let his truth make its full and proper impact on one's mind and heart."[5] In contrast to Eastern meditation, which seeks to empty the mind, Christian meditation seeks to focus and fill the mind with the truth of God.[6]

- *Write:* Author Joan Didion once said, "I write entirely to find out what I'm thinking."[7] Similarly, an adage goes, "There is no impression without expression, and there is no expression without impression." It is vitally important to journal your thoughts. What do you see in God's Word? How will you apply what you have learned? Articulating these thoughts will help them stick. Another benefit is that you can look back over your entries and see how God is working in your life.

- *Closing prayer:* At the end of my quiet time, I thank God for his Word, tell him what I have learned, and seek his help to apply it to my life.

These elements are not necessarily a method but rather practices I have developed during my over forty-year walk with the Lord. My daily

quiet time is a foundational discipline. Whether in times of trouble or
bounty, I can set my eyes on the Lord. I gain wisdom, encouragement,
and hope. I value this time more than any other. Honestly, sometimes
it is drudgery, but most times it is the most wonderful part of my day!
The key is to build a habit. If you do this, God will use his Word to shape
your thoughts, beliefs, and actions. He will change you. And in changing you, he will change the world.

THE FOUR RIGHTS OF THE BIBLE

When we make a habit of meeting God during our quiet time, we will
find that he starts discipling us in four specific areas of thought and
action. In his commentary on the book of Proverbs, Warren Wiersbe
lists the "four rights of the Bible," which are four ways that the Bible
profits believers.[8] In other words, if you read the Bible and put its words
into practice, you will gain wisdom for your decision-making as a disciple and as a leader. Those four "rights" are as follows:

- *What is right* (teaching and doctrine): The Bible is God's essential
  means to teach truth, morality, and wisdom. Through the Holy
  Spirit's help, we are enlightened to God's ways and can compre-
  hend the Bible's teachings. The Bible enables us to discern truth
  from lies, know right from wrong, and exercise good judgment.
- *What is not right* (reproof and conviction): As we read Scripture,
  it helps us see who we really are in light of God. It points to our
  obedience or lack thereof. Painfully at times, it exposes our sinful nature, and it helps us sense God's displeasure with our sinful actions until we confess and repent. When we do confess and
  repent, God restores our fellowship with him, and we continue
  growing in discipleship.
- *How to be right* (correction and discipline): The Bible instructs us
  how to think, feel, and act according to God's will. It shapes our
  minds, hearts, and actions and puts us on the path toward growth
  in godliness and righteousness.
- *How to stay right* (training in righteousness): God's Word provides

instructions and training on how to live a godly life. It provides direction for our priorities, our relationships, our work, and our use of money. It shows us what to avoid, like sexual impurity, drunkenness, pride, and other sins that separate us from fellowship with God.

God's Word is profitable and beneficial. It is living and active. Reading it is like hearing directly from God—his thoughts, his will, his ways. Once you begin reading and applying his Word, God will grow and equip you to help him advance his kingdom.

God is not in need of more people who know the Bible; he desires followers who **apply** *what the Bible says to their everyday lives.*

I love how Josh McDowell puts it: "God changes the lives of those who take his Word to heart. . . . If you ask him to take control of your life, just watch how your attitudes and actions will change, because Jesus—the one who is at the center of everything in the Bible—is in the business of forgiving sin, removing guilt, changing people from the inside out, and healing relationships."[9]

THE "DBDAE" DECISION-MAKING FRAMEWORK

Applying God's Word to your life changes everything, including the way you see yourself and the way you treat others. The Bible takes your eyes off yourself and puts them on God, who, in turn, uses you to change your family, your church, your community, your place of commerce, your political landscape, and your culture. God is not in need of more people who know the Bible; he desires followers who *apply* what the Bible says to their everyday lives. He seeks believers who walk the talk.

One of the most vital leadership areas where you need God's wisdom is in your decision-making. How you make decisions is crucial to developing trust, enhancing your credibility, expanding your influence, and delivering results. The key is to seek divine input before, during, and after making decisions or solving problems. As you soak in God's Word during this process, he will infuse you with knowledge, insight, discernment, understanding, and wisdom.

So what exactly does it look like to make sound decisions? Let's explore a five-step "DBDAE" decision-making framework: (1) define, (2) brainstorm, (3) decide, (4) act, and (5) examine the results.

Define

Successful decision-making begins with plainly describing what's to be considered and then building a boundary of meaning. To do this, write a problem statement. Why should you do this? Because you'll know what you think if you read what you write.

I recommend this problem-statement formula:

- Currently (summary of the situation).
- As a result (consequences).
- We can expect (benefit).

Currently (summary of the situation)

Examine your set of circumstances. What is your specific challenge? How did you arrive in your position? What is wrong or can be improved? What is the gap between where you are now and where you want to be? What is important? Gather as much data as possible to help shape your understanding.

As a result (consequences)

Describe the situationally driven outcomes. What is the impact of the challenge you face? Maybe it is low productivity, excessive waste, higher costs, defective products, or decreased traffic. Regarding people, perhaps it is broken trust or low morale. Or individually, what about emotional, mental, physical, or spiritual tolls? What will happen if the problem continues and is not solved?

We can expect (benefit)

Look to the future and anticipate what will happen if the problem is appropriately addressed. Set a goal. What will be the new result? How will it help you, others, and your organization? What will it look like if you close the gap between where you are and where you want to be? Why is the problem significant to solve?

For example:

- *Currently*, I am not closing sales because I lack the skills necessary to perform my job.
- *As a result*, I am not earning the income I need to support my family, and I am the lowest-producing salesperson on the team.
- *I can expect* that if I develop professional selling skills, I will meet or exceed my income needs by the end of the year and become one of the highest-producing salespeople on the team.

Brainstorm

Once you have written your problem statement, you need to think deeply about the problem at hand and generate solution options.

How do you rack your brain and come up with potential breakthrough solutions? Having grounded yourself in Scripture to align yourself with God's wisdom, values, and creativity, follow these three steps.

Establish your criteria

Before making a decision, you need to define the conditions by which the potential solutions will be evaluated. Think in terms of absolutes and desirables. If something is absolute, the criteria must be met, and no compromise will be made. If something is desirable, the conditions may or may not be met. Absolutes are the must-have solutions, and desirables are solutions with room for compromise.

Brainstorm multiple options

John Steinbeck says, "Ideas are like rabbits. You get a couple and learn how to handle them, and pretty soon you have a dozen."[10] Using your creative thinking skills, brainstorm as many ideas or options as possible.

Start with one or two ideas, let them play off one another, and you will find they begin to multiply. When I am alone and need to come up with several ideas, I take a blank piece of paper, write the problem statement in the middle, and jot down everything that comes to mind, whether words or phrases. I treat each idea as equal and valuable. Even if the idea is absurd, I write it down. Quantity is more important than quality. The more options you have, the greater the chance of making the right decision. Then I group similar ideas into affinity clusters.

You can do the same exercise with a team and a virtual whiteboard or flip chart. Breakthrough ideas are generated when a group of people with diverse backgrounds, thinking styles, and experiences collaborate together. Before you know it, you will have a rabbit colony.

Carefully consider options

Now, compare your options to the decision criteria. How many of them meet the absolute conditions? Of the absolutes, which options stand out by meeting the desirable conditions as well? Lastly, rank the options in terms of effectiveness, difficulty, risk, and future implications. Think about the following questions:

- What will be the impact of this option?
- What is the execution cost of this option?
- What is the risk level of this option?
- If this option is implemented, what will the positive and negative consequences be?

If you establish decision criteria, generate multiple options, and carefully consider all the options, you will be on your way to making sound decisions and solving difficult problems.

Decide

Decisions follow an 80-20 rule. Eighty percent of your choices are recurring every day, like what to wear or where to eat. Twenty percent of your decisions are significant, like choosing whom to marry, changing careers, moving to a new city, or buying a house. With significant decisions, you are typically in novel situations, and you need a thoughtful process to make a quality choice.

Once you have clearly defined the decision to be made or problem to be solved and carefully brainstormed your options, it is time to decide. I recommend following this nine-point checklist for making sound decisions:

1. *Identify values and guiding principles.* Will the chosen option be congruent with your core values and guiding principles? Does it align with the heart of God as revealed in Scripture? Will it honor God and benefit you and others? Why or why not?

2. *Gather information.* Do you have all the information you need to make a quality decision? What's missing? You will never have perfect data, let alone all of it. Glean insights from the data, but do not get stuck in analysis paralysis.

3. *Consider the timing.* When should you make the decision? How urgent and important is the decision? Recall the well-known phrase, "What is important is seldom urgent and what is urgent is seldom important."[11] The level of urgency and importance should drive your decision timing. Do you need to make a choice now? Or can it wait? Why? What is the cost of delaying or not deciding?

4. *Think ahead.* What will the future be like after you decide? After one year, three years, even five years? I recommend writing a brief story about the expected result. Use your imagination. This will help you articulate expectations and develop a clear picture of success. Also, think ahead about scenarios where things may go awry, and then develop contingency plans to correct course if needed.

5. *Involve others.* Determine who needs to participate in the decision-making process. Engage people who have experience with an issue or problem similar to what you face. Seek diverse thoughts and opinions from your family members, peers, team members, and mentors. Try to engage those with different perspectives. This will help reduce your bias, gain clarity, and earn support. I recommend involving two to six people in this process—any more than six will result in diminishing returns.

6. *Create metrics.* When possible, attach qualitative and quantitative measures to your decision. A well-known saying in management is that "what gets measured gets managed."[12] Metrics will help you understand your progress once the decision is implemented in terms of success, failure, or opportunity to correct course.

7. *Write it down.* Transferring a decision from your mind to the written word will increase commitment and establish the foundation from which the results will be measured. Also, articulate your decision rationale. Why did you make this decision? The explanation and metrics will help you evaluate the decision post-implementation.

8. *Make the call.* Decide. Given the conditions, choose which option has the best chance of success based on the parameters you identified and the advice you received.

9. *Overcommunicate.* Share the decision publicly and often. Tell people what was decided and why. You want them to buy into the decision. If people understand the rationale behind the decision—the why—they will be more likely to support its execution. Conversely, the less people understand the why, the less likely they will support implementation.

Act

In the Bible, James states that faith—what is underneath—is dead if there isn't any action (James 2:14–26). Without action, there is no tangible evidence of what we believe. John Calvin says, "It is faith alone that justifies, but faith that justifies can never be alone."[13] Living faith is expressed by deeds of Christian love. Love acts. It cares for orphans and widows. Faith produces proof more than mere words. It produces action.

> *In all our decisions, especially in the workplace,*
> *we should be putting our faith into action.*

What does this have to do with decision-making? Everything. As faith is dead without action, no decision is actually made until it is carried out. And in all our decisions, especially in the workplace, we should be putting our faith into action.

As a leader, follow four steps to convert a decision into action:

1. Define your objective—what you want to achieve and by when.
2. Develop an implementation plan and break it down into specific tasks.
3. Define who is responsible for accomplishing the tasks. Your role as a leader is to empower the team to implement your direction and provide those responsible with the resources, support, training, and tools to carry out the decision. Consider how to inspire them to convert the decision into action.
4. Monitor progress by setting up routines and milestones with those responsible for converting the decision into action. This will drive accountability and keep the lines of communication open. In your meetings, recognize wins, share best practices, and discuss learnings.

Not all decisions are good decisions, and not all good decisions are executed well. If the decision objective is not being met, consider course correction, or make the hard call of abandoning implementation.

Examine the Results

Sometimes you make the right decision and sometimes you do not. But you will only know which is which if you take time to examine the results of a decision. The ancient Greek philosopher Socrates famously said, "The unexamined life is not worth living."[14] He was referring to living under the tyranny of the urgent and never considering the meaning of life. Playing off his quote, I say, "The unexamined decision isn't worth making." Many leaders invest time in the decision-making process, convert the decision to action, and then keep moving. They do not look back, examine the results, or test the outcomes. From my experience, I believe a very high percentage of leaders do not reflect on what worked or did not work and why. Without going the extra mile to examine the consequences of their decisions, leaders miss the opportunity to build upon successes, learn from failures, or correct their course.

To examine a decision, ask these four questions:

1. Did I define the original problem correctly?
2. Did I choose the correct solution?
3. Did I select the correct solution but implement it improperly?
4. Has the implemented solution had ample time to succeed?

The examined decision is worth making. If you invest time scrutinizing your decision outcomes, results, and consequences by reflecting upon these four questions, you will discover areas where you did well or messed up. If you apply your learning to future decisions, you will grow in wisdom, continuously improve, and make sound decisions.

Leaders face countless decisions in the workplace, at home, and in their communities. To make wise decisions as both leaders and disciples of Christ, we need to root ourselves in God's character, values, and promises as revealed in Scripture. By making a daily appointment with God to seek his wisdom, you will find yourself changed day by day to become more like him. This deep-seated change will not just affect your relationship with God; the ripple effect will also cause your connection to him to flow out to those around you. Once changed, you will witness your other relationships change. You may see your culture at work change. But none of that can happen unless you allow God to change you first.

As a disciple, invest time with God. As a leader, seek God when making decisions.

Had I been daily in the Word and seeking God's wisdom when Hunter presented us with what I thought was a once-in-a-lifetime opportunity, I have to think I would have heard and heeded God's still small voice—and Carla's not-so-still-and-not-so-small voice.

QUESTIONS

- Where do you find wisdom? Why is wisdom crucial in leadership?
- When did you last seek God's direction? What happened?
- What happened when you did not seek God's direction?
- If you do not have a daily quiet time, how and when will you cultivate it and make it a habit?
- How do you currently make decisions? How can you begin to use the DBDAE decision-making framework to help you make sound decisions?
- How will these discipleship and leadership principles help you transform your workplace through your pursuit of Christ?

CHAPTER TWO

LOVE

*As a disciple, love God and others
with all you've got.*

As a leader, give up without giving up.

For God so greatly loved and dearly prized the world that He
[even] gave up His only begotten (unique) Son, so that whoever
believes in (trusts in, clings to, relies on) Him shall not perish
(come to destruction, be lost) but have eternal (everlasting) life.

—JOHN 3:16 AMPC

MY DAD IS a rocket scientist—seriously.

In 1996 my dad and mom started a technology business because he and a small team of people had developed a method to track and locate multiple space, air, and ground objects in support of national defense. As the company grew, my dad hired someone to handle the business side, allowing him to focus on the many technological aspects of what his team was accomplishing.

Their partnership flourished. Revenue skyrocketed and their number of employees boomed. My father's expectations were exceeded. He was thrilled with his hire—until he wasn't.

Growth tends to come with growing pains. My dad and his business partner began to differ in their perspectives on the company's direction, even to the point of potentially splitting the well-formed business.

Since I was a minority owner, I had a vested interest in keeping the company afloat and together. And since my father and his business partner believed I could be an impartial judge, they asked me to step in and help resolve their issues. Their request made sense: I had heard both of their arguments for months. Reluctantly, I accepted their invitation to help, but I knew that reconciling two strong-willed men would be challenging. They were similar in many ways—including stubbornness.

In our first official meeting they aired their grievances. Since my dad was the founder and senior member in the room, I ceded the floor to him first. He laid out everything I had already heard: where he thought the company needed to go, what they needed to be focusing on.

After my father finished, I didn't say anything. A pregnant pause hung in the air, then I turned to his business partner and asked, "Well, brother, what do you think about what Dad just said?"

That's when my dad's business partner—his son and my younger brother—shared a different point of view.

WHY MOTIVE MATTERS

It does not take a rocket scientist to figure out that working with family can present unique challenges. (Maybe that's why they brought me in.)

Sure, I wanted to keep the company together, but that was not remotely close to my primary motivation for helping. One of my core values is family. I love my family, and whenever conflict arises, I desire restoration, healing, and peace. I helped my father and brother because I loved them and wanted to keep our family together.

Still, the businessman in me also wanted to figure out how to allow the business to grow and simultaneously protect Dad's interests. So I prayed. I asked God to heal their relationship, and I prayed that I might honor the Lord in my engagement. I also played mediator, talking to them individually and together on conference calls. I listened to both sides, worked hard not to take sides or to make the negotations about me and what I wanted out of them, and focused on solutions.

Then things got really difficult. When we met, our interactions were contentious. I was stuck in the middle, and the issue became a distraction from my full-time job. I was absolutely heartbroken. I wrote in my journal, "I have no solutions. I can only seek God's wisdom." Then I wrote a future headline capturing what I hoped would happen: "Our company posts record earnings, continues to lead innovative solutions, and has the most talented team in the industry. The Poore family, while it went through a rough patch, loves each other and remains whole." I continued, "I beg God that the opposite headline does not come true. Failure, collapse, and demise. God, please moderate hearts, soften them toward one another, and help my family come to an amicable resolution. Reconcile my family and give us peace."

After much prayer, I felt the Lord leading me to disengage as the conflict mediator and encourage my dad and brother to resolve things. I had entered the mediation process even though I knew it would require a sacrifice of time and energy, both personally and professionally, because I love my dad and brother and wanted what was best for them. But at this point, the loving thing for everyone involved was for me to step back and let them talk directly. I told my dad and brother they needed to work out their issues, and I needed to focus on my primary job.

Then something amazing happened: an olive branch appeared. Dad sent my brother an email expressing his desire to keep the company whole and ensure it prospered and maintained its strong talent. They had worked too hard over the years to build the company and did not want to see it fall apart. After reading the conciliatory email, my brother went to my dad's office. They began to talk. Dad also called me and apologized for putting me in the middle of the conflict. He realized it was not fair asking me to take sides, and he recognized the potential long-term damage it would do to the family if I did. He acknowledged that he needed to sacrifice his own agenda to support his sons and to support the flourishing of the whole company.

To make a long and arduous story short, Dad and my brother reconciled. Their relationship was rocky for a while after the cease-fire, but now they are supportive business partners. More importantly, their personal relationship healed as well. They prioritized love over control or getting ahead. And because of their reconciliation, the company is now thriving too.

I recorded in my journal, "God answered my prayer. I didn't come up with the solution through some type of masterful negotiation. God intervened. Thank you, Lord." With God's help, we put our family first. We got the business thrown in. If we had been selfish or partial or had put the business first, we could have lost both.

During the entire process, I learned how important *motive* is to leading others. Motives matter. Motives are the why behind what we do and how we do it. When I helped my father and brother, my motivation was pure: I desired to keep my family together. That untethered motivation helped me lean into the conflict with integrity and selfless ambition, which ultimately aided the company's success. That motivation also helped me navigate conflicts and, with God's help, release my dad and my brother to God so they could work out their relationship directly.

In fact, my motivation was not so much family as something much deeper, something essential to the notion of family.

I was motivated by love.

THE INCREDIBLE STORY OF MAX AND FRANK

As a disciple, love God and others with all you've got. To love God and others like this means you have to be willing to sacrifice. While *sacrifice* is a word we throw around in our churches and workplaces, the story of Max and Frank, prisoners at Auschwitz in 1942 during the Holocaust, helps us understand the ultimate meaning of sacrifice.

The men were forced to live in old, uninsulated brick barracks lacking heat and sanitary restrooms. Leaky roofs dampened the overcrowded buildings. Their straw mattresses became foul because of rampant diarrhea. Bathing water was in short supply. The barracks were full of rats and other disease-spreading rodents. The men received little to eat or drink—a cup of imitation coffee in the morning and weak soup with bread after a long day's work. The captives expended more calories than they consumed, resulting in slow starvation.[1]

Beyond the inhumane conditions was the perpetual fear of beatings, isolation, and execution, a fear that drove some to attempt escape. The Auschwitz concentration camp had a rule that if one prisoner escaped, ten men would be killed in retribution. In July 1941 a man from Max's bunker escaped, and ten men were led out of the bunker to face the Nazi guards. They were threatened with detainment without food or water until they died. Every man trembled with fear. An excruciating death was inevitable.

Frank, imprisoned for helping the Polish resistance, was among the ten men. In a sudden panic, he tearfully appealed to the commandant for his life. "What will my wife and children do?"

Max, who was not among the ten men, observed Frank's impassioned plea and silently stepped forward. Shocked, the commandant demanded to know what Max wanted. Max said, "I want to go instead of the man who was selected. He has a wife and family. I am alone. I am a Catholic priest." Max said he was elderly, although he was only forty-seven. Frank was forty-one.[2] No one knows what went through the commandant's mind, but he did agree to Max's request. Frank returned to the ranks, and Max took his place.[3] Franciscan priest Maximilian (Max) Kolbe suffered starvation and was executed via lethal injection on August 14, 1941. His death allowed Franciszek (Frank) Gajowniczek to live.

What became of Frank? After being released from the concentration camp, he went home to his wife. Unfortunately, his two sons had been killed in the war. Frank never forgot what Father Kolbe did for him, later recalling, "I could only thank him with my eyes. I was stunned and could hardly grasp what was going on. The immensity of it: I, the condemned, am to live and someone else willingly and voluntarily offers his life for me—a stranger. Is this some dream?"[4] In fact, Frank "spent much of his life after World War II bearing witness to the sacrifice made for him by Father Kolbe. He traveled across Europe and the United States, giving talks about the priest and helping dedicate new churches in his name."[5]

Until his death in 1995 at the age of ninety-five, Frank went back to Auschwitz every year to honor Father Kolbe and remember the man who'd sacrificed his life for his own. Because of one man's deep love, another man received fifty-three years of life.

That is love that's given all it's got.

This great act of substitution, of exchanging one's life for another, of bearing the penalty and dying in someone's place, is what Jesus Christ did for you. While we were still sinners worthy of death, God demonstrated his love for us by substituting his Son for us. Greater love has no man than giving his life for another (John 15:13). This is our model—and yet we often strive so hard to give up so little in comparison. We struggle to love God and others better than we currently do. Think about it. How easily would you give your life to save a stranger's? In the words of the apostle Paul, we do not do what we want to do, and instead we do the thing we hate (Rom. 7:15). There is a reason for this, and it goes back to the dawn of creation.

WHY WE STRUGGLE TO LOVE GOD

As a young Christian, I wrestled with a question central to my faith: Why did Christ die for me? Exploring the answer to this question both confirmed my need for the gospel and taught me the true meaning of love and sacrifice.

With this question gnawing at my heart, I began looking for the answer in the Bible. What I learned was basic Christian theology that I think most Christians need to remember—or understand for the first time.

Christ died for us because God is simultaneously holy and loving. We are sinful and helpless, yet he loves us still. Let's look more closely at each of these aspects.

- *God is holy.* J. I. Packer says the term *holy* "signifies everything about God that sets him apart from us and makes him an object of awe, adoration, and dread to us."[6] In other words, if you were to place God next to any human or any other created thing, you would instantly know who was God and who was not.
- *God is love.* At its core, this love is self-giving and self-sacrificial. The Bible describes love this way:

Love never gives up. Love cares more for others than for self. Love doesn't want what it doesn't have. Love doesn't strut, doesn't have a swelled head, doesn't force itself on others, isn't always "me first," doesn't fly off the handle, doesn't keep score of the sins of others, doesn't revel when others grovel, takes pleasure in the flowering of truth, puts up with anything, trusts God always, always looks for the best, never looks back, but keeps going to the end. Love never dies. (1 Cor. 13:4–8 MSG)

- *God is holy* and *loving.* These two character traits seem to compete with each other in a tremendous paradox. How can someone so "set apart" bring others close to him? His holiness demands justice, but his love longs for reconciliation. What happens when the people he loves—his creation, his very sons and daughters—openly rebel against him?

- *We are sinful.* The chief problem of humanity is sin. The Bible says, "All we like sheep have gone astray; we have turned—every one—to his own way" (Isa. 53:6). Although God created people in his image without sin and in perfect relationship with him, every human has been corrupted by sin. Why? Our history of sin began in the garden of Eden.

Adam and Eve disobeyed a direct order from God and ate of the fruit of the tree of the knowledge of good and evil (Gen. 3). Ultimately, they sinned out of their ambition to be like God. Physical death did not come immediately, but a spiritual death did. The once-perfect pair became corrupted, impure, and unholy.

The consequences of Adam and Eve's sin were threefold: the couple's fellowship with God was broken, they became slaves to sin, and every human is born into sin. The Bible tells us that "none is righteous, no, not one; no one understands; no one seeks for God. All have turned aside; together they have become worthless; no one does good, not even one" (Rom. 3:10–12).

As James M. Efird writes, "According to the biblical writers, sin is an ever-present reality that enslaves the human race and has corrupted God's created order. . . . The most basic [definition for *sin*] is a Hebrew word meaning 'revolt' or 'transgression' and indicating a deliberate act of defiance against God. . . . All sin is an act of idolatry, the attempt to replace the Creator with someone or something else, usually one's own self or one's own creation."[7] While the concept of sin can seem intangible, theologian John Stott explains that our sin is demonstrated through "our irrationality, our moral perversity, our blurring of sexual distinctives and lack of sexual control, the selfishness that spoils our family life, our fascination with the ugly, our lazy refusal to develop God's gifts, our polluting and spoiling the environment, the antisocial tendencies that inhibit true community, our proud autonomy, and our idolatrous refusal to worship the living and true God."[8]

Sin ruins us through and through. We would rather be our own god than worship the one true God, and we suffer the consequences of that idolatrous choice. Enslaved to sin, we cannot free ourselves from the predicament in which we each were born. We are all guilty with no way to right our own wrongs (Rom. 3:23). We cannot save ourselves, but God's law requires that we, as morally responsible agents, be held accountable for our sins (Rom. 6:23). Yet such self-justification is impossible. How could even the best judge on earth impartially judge himself? Neither can we earn our justification, our status of being set right with God. The Bible confirms our dire situation when it says, "For by works of the law no human being will be justified in his sight, since through the law comes knowledge of sin" (Rom. 3:20).

Yet we are God's creation, and he loves us. We are the most valued creatures of all because we "are the crown of God's creative activity . . . that he made male and female in his own image."[9] New Testament writers often use the phrase "children of God" to describe Christians. The apostle John says, "See what kind of love the Father has given to us, that we should be called *children of God*; and so we are" (1 John 3:1, emphasis added), and "But to all who did receive him, who believed in his name, he gave the right to become *children of God*, who were born, not of blood nor of the will of the flesh nor of the will of man, but of God" (John 1:12–13, emphasis added). There is a reason God calls himself "Father"—he loves us as only a perfect father can.

So, if God is a holy and loving Father, yet we are his inherently rebellious children, how can the relationship be reconciled? The Father has to do something, and the children have to believe that the Father is acting in their best interest.

What our Father God did was sacrifice his Son on our behalf—the central event of Christianity and maybe its most controversial. How does such an outlandish solution make sense? That requires some Old Testament knowledge.

In the books of the Bible written before Jesus's time, blood symbolized life. Shedding blood equaled death. When the Israelites sinned, God ordered them to sacrifice animals. Often, a lamb was sacrificed on behalf of a sinner, and the lamb's blood was sprinkled on the person to cover him as a sign of righteousness, that is, of being in a right relationship with God.

This ancient sacrificial system that God ordained is known as the old covenant (or promise), and it pointed to the new covenant, which ful-filled the old covenant in the death and resurrection of Jesus. The old covenant was inadequate for people in three ways:

- The sacrifices had to be repeated.
- The sacrifices only externally covered sins. They did nothing to change the "inner person," the heart.
- The sacrifices were not "equally appropriate"[10]—a lamb is not the same as a man.

To satisfy God's wrath, *he* had to be the one to make the offering. Only God could satisfy his own holy requirements. God's appeasement required a substitute who was an appropriate, perfect equivalent. God could have left us to our own fate, eternally separated from him and banished to hell. But because he loves us, he offered his own Son, Jesus, to bear the penalty and die for our sins.

Jesus was sinless, yet he was made sin for us (2 Cor. 5:21). He was God's sacrificial lamb. He shouldered the penalty of our sin. Jesus redeemed us from the law's curse by becoming a curse for us. Because of this, the penalty for our sins was transferred to Jesus as he substituted his life for ours.[11] Because of Jesus's shed blood, those who believe in him and receive him as Lord and Savior are forgiven their sins, given a new heart, and their lives are transformed.

Christ's sacrifice on the cross changed God's dealing with us: he for-gave us. We were justified, redeemed, and reconciled to God. We received his grace: a free gift, unmerited favor. We are at peace with him, no lon-ger alienated from him. Again, John Stott explains:

> Christians can no longer think of themselves only as "created and fallen," but rather "created, fallen and redeemed." . . . For we have not only been created in God's image, but re-created in it. . . . Indeed, every person who is in Christ "is a new creation" (Eph 4:24; Col 3:10; 2 Cor 5:17). This means that our mind, our charac-ter and our relationships are all being renewed. We are God's chil-dren, Christ's disciples and the Holy Spirit's temple. . . . We belong

to the new community which is the family of God. The Holy
Spirit enriches us with his fruit and gifts. And we are God's heirs,
looking forward with confidence to the glory that will one day
be revealed. Becoming a Christian is a transforming experience.[12]

Through Jesus's sacrifice, God makes us holy. He welcomes us into his
presence. We can be his children, without regret, without remorse, without fear. Knowing that so much has been done on our behalf, understanding the profound and life-changing depths of God's sacrifice to
love us—seeing that Jesus is the Max to our Frank—ought to make us
love God all the more. And when we love God first, we love others better.

> *God loves you, so Christ died for you. Not,*
> *Christ died for you so God would love you.*

Frank's response to the great, sacrificial love shown to him by Max
is a challenge to us. He devoted his life to the memory of Father Kolbe.
Because he had been shown such deep love, Frank showed deep love to
others and to the one who'd given his life in Frank's place.

God's love motivates your love. God's sacrifice for you allows you to
sacrifice for others. You are not likely to have to give up your life, but you
will be asked to give up much. How you serve others can define who you
are as a disciple of Christ.

SIX WAYS TO LOVE GOD AND OTHERS

God's motive for loving you isn't flip-flopped: God loves you, so Christ
died for you. Not, Christ died for you so God would love you. God put
his plan of salvation in play *because* he loves you! Jesus gave his life that
you might have a new, everlasting, and abundant life.

As a disciple of Christ, what is your response to God's generous and
magnificent love? Consider the guidance Jesus gave when asked which
of God's commandments are most essential: "The most important is,

'Hear, O Israel: The Lord our God, the Lord is one. And you shall love the Lord your God with all your heart and with all your soul and with all your mind and with all your strength.' The second is this: 'You shall love your neighbor as yourself.' There is no other commandment greater than these" (Mark 12:28–31).

The greatest thing we can do with our lives is to love God and love others with everything we have.

How can we love God? By honoring Christ's sacrifice with a sacrifice of our own—just like Frank made sacrifices throughout his life to repay the unpayable sacrifice Father Max Kolbe made on his behalf. You love God through the daily sacrifice of unreserved surrender and obedience, willingly trading your life for his. In the exchange, your life will be marked by self-denial, taking up the cross daily by the power of the Holy Spirit. As a result, the Holy Spirit will move you toward being more like Jesus—a process called sanctification, "growing in holiness and becoming Christlike."[13]

To grow in holiness, consider these practical ways to love God:

- *Live for God.* Living for God means that you have a wholehearted devotion to him and his ways. You demonstrate your love through obedience—putting your faith into action. Jesus says, "If you love me, show it by doing what I've told you" (John 14:15 MSG). In the Sermon on the Mount, Jesus exhorts his followers to be gentle, show mercy, promote peace, hunger for righteousness, and do good to those who hate us (Matt. 5).
- *Let go and let God.* Relinquish your self-sufficiency and rely on God to control your life and circumstances. Demonstrate your love for him by dropping your guard and being vulnerable. Get out of your own way. Instead of making decisions based on what will be most comfortable or easiest for you, be open to hearing what God wants. Know that he's got your back. Leave the results to him, knowing he works for your best and his honor. If you do, you will be amazed at what he does.
- *Lift praise to God.* Express your deepest love, respect, and appreciation to God. Worship him, not only with your words but with

your life. Louie Giglio, lead pastor of Passion City Church, says, "Worship is our response to what we value most. . . . As a result, worship determines our actions, becoming the driving force for all we do."[14] Discipled leaders value God and all that he has done in their life, and they lift a heart full of praise and worship to God. However you worship—whether through things such as music, enjoying God's creation, or artistic expression—make a practice of showing your awe and thankfulness to God.

However, be warned: Your faith in Jesus will create the desire to serve God and do many things in his honor called "works." Your works are a by-product of your faith in God and your service to him. They do not earn you a better standing with God. These works include being a living sacrifice, praise, worship, prayer, doing good deeds, and sharing your faith with others. But you are not saved by your works. You are saved only by faith in Jesus. In other words, love God and be intentional about growing in holiness, but make sure your motivation is serving God and not serving self by making yourself feel holier.

Sacrifice is the heart of leadership.
Jesus modeled the way for you to be a sacrificial leader.
Think about the immense costs he paid.

Loving God naturally leads to loving those God created. Most of us may be able to love God, but I am willing to bet we struggle more often with loving others. After all, they are as human as we are—and sometimes more so.

How can you love others with all you've got? As God transforms your life, he will move you from selfish conceit to humble service. He will move you from seeking ambition to seeking sacrifice, from yearning for power to yearning to serve, and from living a life of comfort to suffering for his name's sake. The greatest gift you can give others is to lay down your life—your time, your needs, your desires—for them.[15]

Consider these practical ways to love others:

- *Extend a hand.* Put others first and help them by sacrificially giving of your time, talents, and resources. The Bible says, "Learn to do good. Work for justice. Help the down-and-out. Stand up for the homeless. Go to bat for the defenseless" (Isa. 1:17 MSG). Extend help to someone in need and you will make a difference in their life. Perhaps this means volunteering with a local nonprofit, getting involved in outreach at your church, or investing in extended family members who need Christ in their lives.
- *Encourage a soul.* Inspire others with cheerful words. Build their confidence. Look for the best in others and raise their spirits. The Bible says, "Worry weighs a person down; an encouraging word cheers a person up" (Prov. 12:25 NLT). Discipled leaders encourage others in the face of adversity because they know an encouraged soul can overcome any obstacle. Consider texting or emailing someone God has placed on your heart. Leave a note for someone in your workplace, or speak words of life over someone in your home.
- *Engage a heart.* Connect with others by showing how much you care, not how much you know. Be a friend. The Bible describes good friends as those "who love deeply" and "practice playing second fiddle" (Rom. 12:10 MSG). Intentionally look out for others' interests and not yours. Really listen when people ask for help or need a safe place to vent. Lay down your life for them. If you do, you will engage their hearts and love them well.

When you love God and others, God will transform your life. And you will become more like Jesus in the process.

THE SACRIFICE REQUIRED OF A LEADER

As a disciple, love God and others with all you've got.

As a leader, give up without giving up.

This chapter began with these words. What do I mean?

Sacrificing means denying yourself and giving up things for the benefit of others. It means *not* giving up on the problem or the people involved in the problem. Rather, it means giving up on having your own way. It means seeking the greater good at the cost of self. And that cost, especially for a leader, can be very high.

Jesus's example demonstrates that *sacrifice* is the heart of leadership. Jesus modeled the way for you to be a sacrificial leader. Think about the immense costs he paid. He gave up his heavenly throne to come to earth. He served others rather than being served. He faced the constant demand to heal people, teach the masses, cast out demons, feed thousands, confront the Pharisees, raise the dead, and train his disciples.

Even though Jesus faced enormous daily needs, he remained gritty. He never lost sight of his mission, yet he always accommodated others. Despite many "relational interruptions" on his mission, he still chose to die that we might have eternal life. Jesus gave up without giving up. He sacrificed himself, not just once on a cross but every day, all day. Following his Father's daily will prepared Jesus to make the ultimate sacrifice—becoming the living sacrifice we desperately need.

Consider what Jesus's example teaches us:

- *Serve others.* Jesus tells his disciples that if they want to lead, they need to serve others. He then says, "For even the Son of Man came not to be served but to serve others" (Mark 10:45 NLT). Discipled leaders let go of self and put people first. They empty themselves and want the very best for others. They deny their interests, ambitions, and gratification to help individuals or teams reach their potential. Instead of focusing on their own performance reviews or bonuses, leaders think about how best to support and guide those they supervise. Leaders voluntarily give up time, money, and energy to help others succeed or to improve their well-being. They invest in their team members instead of waiting for their team members to invest in them. Leaders lead by serving, and service requires sacrifice.
- *Understand the cost.* Jesus says, "Those of you who do not give up everything you have cannot be my disciples" (Luke 14:33 NIV). Following Jesus requires that we give up everything we have—including self. Discipled leaders consider the cost and still choose

to sacrifice. When you take on a new assignment or team, think carefully about what you will have to sacrifice to give the team the time and commitment it will need to succeed, and if you are not willing or able to make those sacrifices, do not take on the new responsibility. Sacrificial leaders are not concerned about their image, reputation, or being in the spotlight. They give up money, power, and fame—any possession that possesses them. In return, they gain the abundant life Jesus promised.

- *Keep doing good.* The apostle Paul encourages Christian leaders to continue sacrificing: "Do not become weary or lose heart in doing right [but continue in well-doing without weakening]" (2 Thess. 3:13 AMPC). Leaders forfeit a lot for the benefit of others, and being a leader requires endurance. Pace yourself and recognize your own limits and the need to delegate work so you will not burn out and leave your team without strong direction and leadership. Leaders are asked to give up more and to do so more often than others. Frequent sacrifice requires being gritty like Jesus, showing the staying power to endure the challenge of sacrifice. Leaders maintain the strength of mind to continue denying themselves and helping others. Such discipled leadership is costly and requires God-given resilience.

If you sacrifice without love,
your leadership is worthless.

Through loving and serving others, understanding the costs of sacrifice, and continuing to do good, you will emulate Jesus's example and become a sacrificial leader. But if you sacrifice without love, your leadership is worthless. Remember, God's love motivates your love, and your love can motivate others. To serve and to sacrifice is to show love, but are your actions motivated by his love?

Are you working to save the company—your profits, your career, your reputation—or are you working to save your family, those you love? As my story about mediating for my dad and brother attests, motives—whether you want to promote your own agenda or if you are looking after the collective good of those around you—will drastically change your actions and interactions with others.

Earlier in this chapter, we looked at the "love section" of Paul's first letter to the Corinthians. As we conclude the chapter, consider whether you are motivated by love by replacing the word *love* in this passage with your name. Do the words still hold true?

> Love never gives up. Love cares more for others than for self. Love doesn't want what it doesn't have. Love doesn't strut, doesn't have a swelled head, doesn't force itself on others, isn't always "me first," doesn't fly off the handle, doesn't keep score of the sins of others, doesn't revel when others grovel, takes pleasure in the flowering of truth, puts up with anything, trusts God always, always looks for the best, never looks back, but keeps going to the end. Love never dies. (1 Cor. 13:4–8 MSG)

When leading others, consider this charge:

- *Examine your motive.* Why are you doing what you are doing? Determine if your motive is a selfless desire to bestow value on others. Is your motive genuine and authentic? Are you doing the "right things" to look good and get ahead? If so, you may want to check your motive at the door.
- *Act on your motive.* Serve others and look out for their interests. Help people achieve their goals and reach their potential.
- *Reflect on your motive.* After acting, determine the results and recalibrate your motive if necessary. Learning to lead from the pure motive of love is a lifelong process, not a one-and-done accomplishment.

If you love God with all you've got and follow the steps of examining, acting, and reflecting on your motive, you will be a well-motivated leader.

You can do this. But you have to give up yourself first.
And that's not rocket science.

QUESTIONS

- What motivates you? When in a leadership capacity, how do you examine, act, and reflect on your motives?
- What is the connection between love and leadership?
- Can you name some sacrificial leaders in your life? Maybe a parent, friend, teacher, coach, mentor, or manager? What did they sacrifice to help you? How will you sacrifice to help someone?
- How do we love God and others? Which strategy suggested in this chapter is the most meaningful to you?
- How will these discipleship and leadership principles help you transform your workplace through your pursuit of Christ?

CHAPTER THREE

BELIEVE

As a disciple, take God at his word.

As a leader, cultivate God-confidence.

*And this is the testimony, that God gave us eternal life,
and this life is in his Son. Whoever has the Son has life; whoever
does not have the Son of God does not have life. I write these things
to you who believe in the name of the Son of God, that you may
know that you have eternal life.*

—1 JOHN 5:11–13

MY PASTOR COULD not have been blunter: "Are you trusting God or yourself?"

I put my head in my hands, the picture of a man who felt like giving up. I did not want to uproot my family for the fifth time in eleven years. Plus, I'd promised my two kids they'd graduate from their current high school.

We had been in Knoxville for six years, the longest we had stayed in one place. We lived in a beautiful home, had great friends and neighbors, served at our church, attended University of Tennessee football games, and had spent many days boating on Lake Louden.

But then 2009 came for us with a vengeance, just like it did for millions across the country. During the Great Recession, the company I worked for acquired another large company. Because of the acquisition and related organizational changes, they eliminated my role in Knoxville. The good news was that the company offered me another role. The bad news was that accepting the position meant relocating for the fifth time in my career, this time to Atlanta—more than two hundred miles away from Knoxville. The worse news was that my new job would require breaking my promise to my family.

I was disheartened. I had made a pledge to them and was so close to fulfilling it. My daughter was beginning her senior year in high school, my son had just started his freshman year, and my wife was deeply rooted in the community. I was determined to keep my word. I put on a full-court press looking for another job in Knoxville. I was willing to take a pay cut and do anything to remain in Knoxville and stay true to my promise.

I invested hours into contacting executive recruiters and mining job opportunities. Eventually, I connected with a recruiter who helped me secure an interview with a Knoxville-based consumer products company. My background, experience, and personality were a great fit. Over two days, I interviewed with eighteen people. I drove to Atlanta to take a battery of tests and participate in a psychological evaluation. I believed the interview process was going well and everything was falling into place. I would be able to keep my promise.

Then the recruiter called to say I had not gotten the job. I was shocked, then I was crushed, then I was shocked again. I got on my knees and cried and prayed to God. Every door was closed, every opportunity exhausted. I only had two choices: stay in Knoxville without a job or take the opening in Atlanta.

> *The central question of confidence for the discipled leader is . . . "Are you trusting God or yourself?"*

I did not know what to do. That's when I reached out to my pastor for counsel, and he said, "Maybe you're overvaluing the stability of staying put. Are you trusting God or yourself?"

Conviction washed over me. My family's flourishing was not dependent on my expectations for our future or my ability to prove myself. My two choices were not really about whether to relocate. My two choices were to trust myself or trust God.

BELIEVE GOD'S WORD

Discipled leaders take God at his word. When I was struggling about what job to take and where my family should live, I was not being a discipled leader. I was being a self-led leader. Why? Because I was not placing my confidence in the only One who controls everything.

The central question of confidence for the discipled leader is the same question my pastor asked me: "Are you trusting God or yourself?" In what or whom do you place your confidence? Your résumé? Your spouse? Your title? Your boss? Your tenure? Your intelligence?

Self-confidence means relying on your abilities, experience, and accomplishments to achieve a successful outcome. Self-confidence is the subtle, pervasive lie that you are in control. It is telling God, "I've got this. If it is to be, it's up to me." Self-confidence coupled with success leads to pride. You may think, *Look at who I am and what I've done.* (I certainly have.) But pride and self-reliance inevitably lead to a fall. Events spin out of control. Circumstances turn. Life changes.

Then what? Where do you turn?

Many professing Christians would quickly answer, "I turn to God." But anecdotal evidence, at least from my own life, reveals that is not always the case. In difficult circumstances, we often try to be good Christians in our own strength, but we run out of steam and fall back into old behavior patterns. We give up on taking God at his word and fall back on every human's default mode of operation: self-confidence. We live like we are unaware of God's safety net. If we only truly understood what God offers us, we would be able to withstand the worries, pressures, and temptations of this world.

Maybe an illustration will help.

THE BRIDGE

Naysayers said for years that a bridge could not be built connecting the two peninsulas. Considered one of the most challenging stretches of water in the world, its expanse is 6,700 feet wide and is five hundred feet deep at its center. The tides that move in and out of the bay create strong, cold, swirling currents. Heavy winds gusting up to seventy-five miles per hour flare up when the air is forced up the surrounding hills. As if all that were not bad enough, fog blankets the area when the winds die down, resulting in zero visibility. These conditions made it seem impossible to build such a bridge.[1]

Enter Joseph Strauss. He saw what others could not: a bridge spanning more than eight thousand feet that would connect two peninsulas and create tremendous economic growth. Strauss worked to remove all

political barriers that stood in the way of fulfilling his dream and gaining the required financial support. The construction plans were drawn,
the materials were purchased, and he was ready to build. But Strauss
needed just one more thing: workers.

Fortunately for Strauss, it was the Great Depression, and most folks
were willing to do anything to make a living. They would even lie about
being ironworkers to get a job. Once hired, the bridge builders faced
treacherous conditions: howling winds, lofty heights, slippery surfaces, dense fog, and a roaring ocean below. One misstep in the unfor-
giving environment meant certain death. For this type of construction
project, the rule of thumb was that for every one million dollars in
cost, one person would die. This great venture was projected to cost
thirty-five million dollars—at the potentially higher cost of thirty-five
lives lost!

Because of the great risk, Strauss needed to provide a secure work
environment, one where workers felt confident that if they fell from a
great height, they would be safe. Strauss wondered what would happen
if the workers had something they could trust to catch them—like a
safety net. He put his idea into motion and invested $130,000 in a huge
net, which was placed under the construction site.

During the project, nineteen workers fell. The safety net—and
Strauss's inventive thinking—saved every worker. Not only did the net
fulfill its sole function of saving lives, but knowing the safety net would
catch them boosted the workers' confidence. As assurance and security
improved, workers willingly sped up their work. They became more productive and effective. Because of the knowledge that a net would catch
them if they fell, the workers risked dire conditions and completed one
of the greatest architectural structures of modern times, the Golden
Gate Bridge.

Just as the Golden Gate Bridge workers trusted that a safety net would
catch them if they fell, so too can you trust God's safety net. The inter-
woven strands of that net are the objective and subjective assurances
of your salvation. In other words, you can trust that God will provide
because his Word says so and your life proves so.

ASSURING YOUR SALVATION

Christians fail to take God at his word in many ways, whether by failing to trust him with relationships, families, jobs, communities, or personal well-being. But at the core of a Christian's doubt about God's safety net—his promise to catch us and love us no matter what (Rom. 8:38-39)—lurks a question that nags every doubter: Am I really saved? When we are assured of God's salvation in our lives, then we know we can trust him with everything else in our everyday experience.

You can know objectively and subjectively that you are saved. You know what *objective* means, but you may have never read a full definition: "Expressing or dealing with facts or conditions as perceived without distortion by personal feelings, prejudices, or interpretations."[2] Through God's Word, we objectively understand salvation:

- *If you believe in Jesus, you are saved.* "For God so loved the world, that he gave his only Son, that whoever believes in him should not perish but have eternal life" (John 3:16). Belief means more than head knowledge. There is a big difference between knowing about someone and actually knowing and having a relationship with someone. Belief moves from the head to the heart where you wholeheartedly surrender your life to Jesus and place your trust in him.
- *Salvation is a gift.* "For by grace you have been saved through faith. And this is not your own doing; it is the gift of God" (Eph. 2:8). Salvation cannot be earned; it is a gift. Through God's worthiness, character, and generosity, he justifies the believer. Your role is to place your faith in him who saves you.
- *You are kept in God's power.* "For I am sure that neither death nor life, nor angels nor rulers, nor things present nor things to come, nor powers, nor height nor depth, nor anything else in all creation, will be able to separate us from the love of God in Christ Jesus our Lord" (Rom. 8:38-39). You are justified by faith in the arms of everlasting love, where no hostile power or conceivable event can ever tear you apart from God.

You can also know subjectively that you are saved. *Subjective* means "modified or affected by personal views, experience, or background."[3] This means that you witness God's transforming power in your life as assurance of his love and his work of redemption. Through the Holy Spirit's power, you experience him shaping your character to reflect Jesus's character. Ask yourself the following questions and consider his work in your life:

- *Do you* believe *God?* This is a doctrinal question. The Bible promises, "Everyone who believes that Jesus is the Christ has been born of God, and everyone who loves the Father loves whoever has been born of him" (1 John 5:1). It is important that you believe Jesus is who he says he is: God's Son in the flesh, Savior, King of Kings, and Lord of Lords.
- *Do you* obey *God?* This is a lifestyle question. The Bible tells us, "By this we know that we love the children of God, when we love God and obey his commandments. For this is the love of God, that we keep his commandments. And his commandments are not burdensome" (1 John 5:2–3). To be sure that you know God, you must keep his commandments.
- *Do you* love *others?* This is a social question. The apostle John writes, "By this we know love, that he laid down his life for us, and we ought to lay down our lives for the brothers" (1 John 3:16). If you lack love for others, you do not have the love of God in your heart.

Genuine assurance of salvation in Christ naturally leads to a steadfast peace in every other area of life.

Assurance is "being certain in the mind."[4] You can be certain in your mind about your salvation. Assurance is confidence that Christ's promise to you—that if you believe in him you will be saved—is true. As Lawrence Richards writes, "God doesn't want us to go through life fearful and uncertain about our relationship with him. . . . We have God's promise. We are his."[5]

Jesus's resurrection from the dead is the pledge God has given that his revelation is true and worthy of acceptance. Why? Jesus is the only person ever to fulfill a promise of dying and rising again. Because of Jesus's fulfilled promise, you can have the "full assurance of faith," a fullness of faith in God that leaves no room for doubt (Heb. 10:22). You can also have the "full assurance of understanding"—that is, an entire, unwavering conviction of the truth of the declarations of Scripture.[6]

Genuine assurance of salvation in Christ naturally leads to a steadfast peace in every other area of life. This assurance also leads to love, thankfulness, resilience, strength, and cheerfulness. Your assurance may be shaken, weakened, or interrupted, but it can never be lost.[7]

GOD-CONFIDENCE: TRUSTING ENOUGH TO OBEY

I rest assured in my salvation objectively because I take God's Word as God's word. I rest assured subjectively because I have seen his hand at work throughout my life—even when I moved my family yet again.

When I heard my pastor's question, "Are you trusting God or yourself?" I put my head in my hands—but I immediately knew my answer. I had been relying on myself, even to the point of being stubborn about my self-led decisions.

Believing that God engineers all circumstances, I surrendered to him at that moment. Even though the future was not clear and it would likely mean another upheaval for my family, I decided to trust God, relying on him because I am confident in his salvation. I know he loves me and will be faithful to his promises to keep and guide me.

I accepted the new role in Atlanta, and we began the relocation process. It was not easy. We sold our house and moved into a rental home so our daughter could finish her senior year in Knoxville. I commuted to Atlanta for a year, living in a hotel during the week and driving home on the weekends. Then we moved to Atlanta. Our son transferred to a new high school in the middle of the year. My wife faced making new friends, again. In the midst of all of our challenges, I journaled many times about not understanding our circumstances but trusting God—trusting that he'd work things out for his glory and our good.

The Poores had long lived by the motto, "Grow where you're planted." Now we had yet another opportunity to apply it. What's more, my wife and I had the opportunity to model for our kids what trusting God really looks like and what it requires.

The decision to put our confidence and future in God's hands shaped my family. I am glad to report that we successfully established roots in Atlanta, and we all grew beyond our imaginations. God has been faithful in every way, even when we doubted.

> *As you surrender your heart to God, you will become a catalyst for God to transform, innovate, and positively influence the world around you.*

Throughout the process, I kept reminding myself why I could trust God with uprooting our comfortable lives: I can take him at his word. Assurance of my salvation provided the God-confidence I needed to drastically change our lives. I knew how he had changed my life before, from the moment of my salvation to every moment after.

While I learned many lessons about cultivating God-confidence instead of self-confidence during this time, I highlight three important ones.

Cultivating God–Confidence Empowers You to Trust Him Completely

The Bible says, "Trust GOD from the bottom of your heart; don't try to figure out everything on your own. Listen for GOD's voice in everything you do, everywhere you go; he's the one who will keep you on track" (Prov. 3:5–6 MSG). Trusting that God has got your back will make a big difference in how you see events in your life unfold. Set your hope and confidence in God's character. Too many of us live like God is far away, inconsistent, or angry, when really God describes himself as merciful, gracious, loving, faithful, forgiving, and just (Exod. 34:6–7). Trust him wholeheartedly with complete surrender. Don't just go halfway. Don't trust God with your time but not with your finances. Don't trust God with your family but not with your work life. Give him everything you have. Do your best not only to know God but also to fear and honor him. Surrender every part of your being to him—your mind, will, and emotions. Embrace the fact that God can do his will. In his wisdom, he knows what is best, and in his love, he will do what is best for you.

Cultivating God-Confidence Helps You Join God in His Kingdom Work

The Bible says, "In their hearts humans plan their course, but the LORD establishes their steps" (Prov. 16:9 NIV). God governs our world and engineers all circumstances. He is in control. So collaborate with him. Join in what he is doing. Wait on him, gain his insight through Scripture, understand what he wants to accomplish, seek his direction in prayer, and *then* move when prompted. As you surrender your heart to God, you will become a catalyst for God to transform, innovate, and positively influence the world around you. God will work in you and through you to bring order from chaos, solve impossible problems, make wise decisions in times of crisis, and move people and resources toward reaching their potential. When you place your confidence in God and his purposes instead of working in your own strength, he will fit you into a work much bigger and more meaningful than you imagined.

Cultivating God-Confidence Makes You Courageous

The Bible says, "God is our refuge and strength, a very present help in trouble" (Ps. 46:1). Trusting God emboldens you to act in the face of difficulty, uncertainty, pressure, or opposition. You more easily move out of your comfort zone and take risks, because you know you can rely on his promise that he will provide strength and protect you in times of trouble. Know and embrace that he is with you and for you; nothing can be against you. He will provide the strength you need to act in the midst of fear.

GOD-CONFIDENCE IN THE WORKPLACE

Legendary NFL coach Vince Lombardi said, "Confidence is contagious and so is lack of confidence."[8] People can tell if you have confidence, and if you don't, they will not follow you. If you do, they will see you as competent, and they will trust and follow you.

The goal is not that Christian leaders exude a worldly, self-centered confidence. What leaders should strive for both personally and professionally is the kind of salvation-assured God-confidence we have been discussing this entire time. This kind of confidence is even more contagious than what Coach Lombardi was talking about.

Discipled leaders learn to elevate God rather than themselves. The Bible says, "Don't be so naive and self-confident. You're not exempt. You could fall flat on your face as easily as anyone else. Forget about self-confidence; it's useless. Cultivate God-confidence" (1 Cor. 10:12 MSG). God-confident leaders seek his strength and protection to face opposition or challenging times. They trust that God will provide a successful outcome—as he defines it. When that success comes, leaders give credit to God.

How different would your life look if you really believed God and walked in faith? How would your company grow? How would your world be transformed? Focusing on God and not on yourself will make your confidence soar, and you will be energized to do and achieve more than you imagined possible.

DANCING INTO THE DISCOMFORT ZONE

Have you ever had one of those moments that made you think, "There's no way I'm going to do that"? I had one on a business trip to meet with a new team in New York City. Part of our agenda was to build comradery through a fun, shared experience. The night before the event, the team seemed very excited about what we were going to do, but they kept the event a secret from me. I am a planner and always like to be ready for what's next. I softly pressed the team about what we were going to do, but they did not budge. All they asked was that I have an open mind and wear some workout clothes.

Early the next morning, we met in the hotel lobby. Everyone else was in their workout clothes, and I thought we would do something like jogging in Central Park. We left the hotel and began walking toward Radio City Music Hall. *This is interesting*, I thought. *I wonder what's up.*

The team leader knocked on a side door, and we were escorted into a dance studio.

I asked the team leader, "This is cool being in Radio City Music Hall, but what are we going to do?"

She replied, "It's always been a bucket list item of mine to dance with the Rockettes. We are going to learn a dance together."

"Awesome!" I said. "It will be fun to watch you all. It sounds like a unique experience."

She smiled. "Watch you all? You're going to dance with us, aren't you?"

I got a lump in my throat. I would rather get a root canal. I love freestyle dance, but I have never been any good at choreographed dances. I am quite possibly one of the clumsiest people around. I was afraid I was going to embarrass myself.

I sheepishly said, "Mind if I sit this one out?"

"Oh, come on, Preston. You can do this, and the team will love you for it."

I was at a decision point. Do I excuse myself, not participate, and watch from the sidelines? Or do I risk the embarrassment, leap in, and connect with the team? Do I stay in my comfort zone or move outside it?

After all this went through my head, I mustered up the courage to dance with the team. "OK, I'll do it. What have I got to lose?"

You know what? I had an absolute blast. Two Rockettes came into the room and taught our nine-member team how to dance "The Parade of the Tin Soldiers" from *The Nutcracker* ballet. It is one of the most famous routines in Radio City Music Hall's Christmas Spectacular. We learned all the dance steps and kicks. It was a great team-building exercise. We laughed a lot and had a great time.

None of this would have happened if I had sat on the sidelines. I had to check my ego at the door and step outside my comfort zone to grow and connect with the team. Initially I was uncomfortable because I had to let go of my self-confidence and sense of control. I was not good at choreography, I did not know what the instructors were going to ask us to do, and I was sure I would end up looking stupid at some point. But then I realized this team-building exercise was not up to me. By putting my confidence in God—the one who orchestrates all things, gave us the good gifts of community and movement, and loves and values me even when I look stupid—I found the courage to put my team first and connect with them over something I could not control.

Cultivating God-confidence gives you the courage to do things outside your comfort zone.

It is important for leaders to step with God-confidence into discomfort zones—places where you are tested or do something new. Several positive results will occur when you do.

- *Your potential will unlock.* Do you wonder why you haven't accomplished more in your life? Do you feel your potential is locked up inside and is screaming to get out? The truth is that no one actually reaches their full potential, and the sad thing is that most people only scratch the surface. The key to unlocking your potential is to make the choice to reach toward it. Be intentional. How? By setting goals, acting boldly, making daily progress, developing habits, and overcoming obstacles. Give your very best every day. If you do, you'll move closer to reaching your potential and begin making a positive impact on those around you.
- *Your perspective will change.* When you muster the courage to engage in a new, different, or possibly embarrassing experience, your mindset will move from "I can't" to "I can," "I won't" to "I will," and "I shouldn't" to "I should."
- *You will grow.* Be a rubber band: it's only useful when it's stretched. Moving out of the safe and secure will stretch your limits; you'll discover new God-given talents, build new skills, and develop new

abilities. Growth occurs in the yet-to-be-experienced moments of life that are outside your normal boundaries.

Cultivating God-confidence gives you the courage to do things outside your comfort zone. He's got you, even if you have two left feet like I do. When you face something new or different, I challenge you to try it. If you do, you will learn and grow as you dance into the discomfort zone. What are you waiting for?

What holds you back from fully placing your faith in Jesus Christ both for the assurance of your salvation and in the day-to-day challenges of your workplace?

As a disciple, take God at his word. As a leader, cultivate God-confidence.

When you do both of these on a regular basis, they will feed into each other, and your faith and confidence in God's plan for your life will only increase—even in times of doubt and worry. If you become confident in God and his grace, you will live effectively for him and be enabled to overcome a world of difficulty. Your confidence in the Lord's salvation promise is fundamental to your walk with him. Imagine what he can do through your life if you trust him, knowing that he is your safety net on this bridge called life.

QUESTIONS

- Are you self-confident or God-confident? How can you cultivate God-confidence in your life?
- If you died in ten minutes, where would your soul go? Why?
- When did you last trust God, embrace change, and experience growth?
- When was the last time you took a risk and stepped out of your comfort zone? What happened? What did you learn?
- How will these discipleship and leadership principles help you transform your workplace through your pursuit of Christ?

CHAPTER FOUR

CONFESS

As a disciple, keep short accounts with God.

As a leader, be honest to the core.

If we [freely] admit that we have sinned and confess our sins, He is faithful and just (true to His own nature and promises) and will forgive our sins [dismiss our lawlessness] and [continuously] cleanse us from all unrighteousness [everything not in conformity to His will in purpose, thought, and action].

—1 JOHN 1:9 AMPC

EVAN, MY CROSS-FUNCTIONAL partner and region president at our multi-billion-dollar consumer products company, stopped me in the parking lot. "Have you noticed how execution's gotten sloppy over the past year?"

I nodded.

He looked down. "Not too long ago, this was one of the best-executing markets. I'm very disappointed. What's happened?"

I paused. I did know what had happened, but for several reasons, the timing hadn't ever been right to tell Evan, until now. I knew that if I told him the truth, there would be consequences. Maybe even for Evan himself. But *integrity* is a word that means something to me, so I mustered up my courage and told him what I knew. "Did you know the local management team is running a side business out of the office?"

Shocked, he just said, "No."

"The local team is focused on building their side business, and they're using company assets for personal gain. They're violating our code of business conduct, and they've lost focus on their primary job responsibilities. That's the reason execution is so sloppy."

I could tell that Evan did not quite believe me, so I walked him over to a manager's company vehicle in the parking lot. "See that?" I pointed to a window decal on the manager's windshield. "That's the logo for their side business."

He shook his head.

"That's just the tip of the iceberg too. If you poke around, you'll probably find out what's going on."

"I will, Preston. I will."

True to his word, Evan poked around. He discovered that the local management team had invented a new sports gadget and were leveraging the company's people, tools, and supplies to build their side business. Over time, they had become so consumed with growing their own business that they had neglected their primary responsibility: marketplace execution.

If questioned about negative business results, the team leaders deflected the inquiries and pointed to factors "outside their control." They disguised their side interest by saying all of the right things to upper management. Consequently, the team was left alone to work on their own business on our company's dime. Eventually, their audio and video did not match. Without accountability, the team had abandoned their integrity and slowly moved into corruption.

After my conversation with Evan, I knew that the circumstances and potential consequences would escalate. I called my manager and told him about the conversation. My manager told human resources and other leaders about the potential code of business conduct violation. Following an investigation, a number of local market leaders were fired for leveraging company assets and personally gaining from their efforts.

I made the right decision even though it was tough and even though I was saddened that a number of employees lost their jobs. But the experience reminded me of the necessity of integrity—with others, with myself, and, most importantly, with God. I learned that when you become a disciple with integrity, you can become a leader others will follow because of your honesty.

A LEADER'S MOST ADMIRED TRAIT

The authors of *The Leadership Challenge* surveyed more than one hundred thousand people on what they looked for and admired most in a leader. Honesty topped the list every time. The authors observed,

> It's clear that if people anywhere are willing to follow someone—
> whether it's into battle or the boardroom, in the front office or

on the production floor—they first want to be sure that the individual is worthy of their *trust*. . . . No matter what the setting, people want to be fully confident in their leaders, and to be fully confident they have to believe that their leaders are individuals of *authentic* character and solid *integrity*.[1]

Honest people admit when they have made a mistake or were wrong—a key ingredient of discipleship.

Honest people speak the truth. They live in reality and prefer facts over fiction. *Honesty* is often used interchangeably with the words *authenticity* and *integrity*. Honesty is also the basis of trust. If you trust what someone does, you will consider that person dependable, reliable, and consistent. You will know what to expect and that you can count on them. Honest people admit when they have made a mistake or were wrong—a key ingredient of discipleship we will soon cover.

People do not want dishonest or deceitful leaders—ones who cheat, lie, or are underhanded. You never know where you stand with them or what may happen. Honesty *is* the best policy! The Bible says, "Honesty guides good people; dishonesty destroys treacherous people" (Prov. 11:3 NLT). Honesty will help you navigate every circumstance without compromising your integrity. Discipled leaders are honest to the core.

People watch leaders to see if they are who they say they are and if they do what they say they will do. Their actions speak louder than their words.

KEEPING SHORT ACCOUNTS

Honesty means being honest with yourself about your strengths, weaknesses, mistakes, and responsibilities—a great definition of *integrity*—and being honest with yourself is critical to being honest with your team.

Being honest with yourself means agreeing with God about your shortcomings. A leader with integrity confesses his or her faults. As a disciple, keep short accounts with God. Be honest about the ways you have fallen short of God's perfect design for you and your life (Rom. 3:23). Admit your mistakes and throw yourself on God's mercy. Only by practicing an awareness of our failures and God's grace will we learn to recognize our sin and live in redeemed relationships with God and the people he has put around us.

In his excellent book *The Man in the Mirror,* Patrick Morley writes,

> When we are all alone, with no peer pressure keeping us on the straight and narrow path, that's when our real character is put to the test. . . . This issue is so important because unless we hold onto absolute integrity in every situation, no matter how big or small, we grieve God and cut ourselves off from the blessing we want and that God wants to give. "Whoever can be trusted with very little can also be trusted with much, and whoever is dishonest with very little will also be dishonest with much" (Luke 16:10).[2]

Disciplined leaders must have integrity before God before they can have integrity before others.

Disciplined leaders must have integrity before God before they can have integrity before others. If disciplined leaders are right with God, they can operate from moral authority. Through God's power, such leaders can straighten what was bent, mend what was broken, and right most wrongs. If a leader is not right with God yet still works for justice, that leader is hypocritical and will ultimately be ineffective. Jesus's words in Matthew 7:1-5 about seeing the speck in someone else's eye before removing the plank in your own come to mind. You cannot be, say, or do something for a long period of time that is different from what is really inside you.

That's where confession comes in.

Confession—honestly admitting our sins to God, repenting and turning away from our sins, and trusting that in God's mercy, he has already paid for our sins on the cross—allows a discipled leader to reconnect with God. Confession restores us to fellowship with the only One who really knows us and with the only One who can really help us know ourselves.

If all these good things happen when we confess, why don't we confess more often?

WHY WE FEAR CONFESSION

We hesitate to confess for any number of reasons, but a chief reason is that we fear God's disapproving glare—or even his banishment. But these are unfounded fears. When you become a parent, nothing will ever change the fact that your child is your child. No matter what they do, your child is still your son or daughter. What happens when your child disobeys and breaks the trust you have both worked so hard to establish? The relationship does not change, but the fellowship does.

John MacArthur puts it this way: "We are still his or her parent, ready to forgive instantly. But until he or she comes to us to *confess* his or her disobedience, the prior intimacy will not be restored."[3] Disobedience disrupts your fellowship with your child until an authentic apology is given and accepted. Consequences and discipline may follow, but unconditional love remains.

Isn't this how we relate to God? Even when we break fellowship with God through sin, God still loves us unconditionally. He still desires fellowship—a special bond and intimacy with us when we walk with God, enjoy his presence, share mutual affection and friendship, know his will, and are aligned with it. He is still our Father in heaven, and he still longs to be close to us.

The problem is not him. It's us. God does not move or go away. We do.

Even though Jesus's death dealt fully with sin, our sin nature is still engrained in us. Our challenge is dealing with the reality of sin in our lives. We continue to experience pride, lust, anger, hate, and distrust of God. We will battle sin's impulses for as long as we have the capacity to sin—that is, until we are in heaven.[4]

When we fail to confess sin regularly, we begin to believe that our sins are justified, that they are not a big deal, or even that we have not really sinned. Lawrence Richards describes what happens when he says, "Closing our eyes to reality, we'll wander through life, insisting on our sinlessness and yet wondering why we have only an aching void inside rather than fellowship's joy."[5]

If you want to get specific about why we fail to approach God in confession more often, consider the following characteristics. If any of them currently exist in your life, you may be past due for an honest prayer of confession.

- *Guilt.* Since you are made in the image of God, you know right from wrong. An act or thought committed against God and others creates a great emotional and spiritual burden in your conscience. Guilt can produce emotions like misery, hopelessness, shame, fear, anxiety, and unworthiness. When you do wrong, you feel the burden of sin until that weight is lifted. King David writes, "When I kept it all inside, my bones turned to powder, my words became daylong groans. The pressure never let up; all the juices of my life dried up" (Ps. 32:3–4 MSG).
- *Accusations.* Satan's accusations pour more shame onto you. After drawing you toward sin, he will point his finger at you, reinforcing the guilt you are experiencing. He will tell you that you are finished, that you have no future with God, and that there is no way back to God. Satan aims to isolate you from God and make you ineffective and unproductive. Ultimately, he wants to destroy you.
- *Alienation.* Breaking fellowship with God leads to a loss of affection for God. With continued and unconfessed sin, you will lose fellowship not only with God but also with your Christian brothers and sisters. You will begin to conform to the pattern of the world and become a willing slave to sin.
- *Slavery.* One "small" sin can incubate into much larger sins that overtake your life. The very thing you know not to do you do because you are influenced more by Satan, the world, and your own flesh than you are by the Holy Spirit.
- *Consequences.* Warren Wiersbe says, "When we deliberately disobey

God, we suffer both from the consequences of our sins and from the chastening hand of God, unless we repent and submit."[6] The Bible warns us against making light of God's justice when it says, "Don't be misled—you cannot mock the justice of God. You will always harvest what you plant. Those who live only to satisfy their own sinful nature will harvest decay and death from that sinful nature. But those who live to please the Spirit will harvest everlasting life from the Spirit" (Gal. 6:7–8 NLT).

When you experience any of these effects of sin, you want to do just the same as a child who has been caught stealing cookies: hide. (Isn't that exactly what Adam and Eve did?) You want to conceal your sin from God, but that inevitably leads to a gradual "moving away from a close walk with Christ into a life filled with the alien world in which we live."[7]

The key is to seek God and his forgiveness when you fall.

In James 1:14–15, the apostle James describes the road markers on the path that veers away from a close walk with Christ:

- *Temptation.* An enticing object is presented that looks good, pleasurable, but is contrary to God's Word.
- *Desire.* The temptation elicits a strong emotional response and intent to act.
- *Sin.* Your desire is carried out through deed or thought. You choose to sin.
- *Death.* Your fellowship with God is blocked.

Notice that being tempted or feeling a desire to do something wrong is not itself sin. Also remember that when you have committed sin, you have the choice to confess it to God and repent, or keep it to yourself. Confession is the fork in the road for every Christian who has ever sinned, which is all of us. When you have walked the path of sin to its inevitable conclusion, you can continue to walk in darkness, or you can veer toward the light. No matter how far you have fallen away, you can find your way back to God through confession.

WHY YOU NEED TO CONFESS

During your Christian journey, you will become polluted by the world. Take heart: this is common for all Christians. You will not lose your salvation or relationship to God as his son or daughter, but you will temporarily lose fellowship with him. Your sins do not separate you from the love of the Father. You are held in his hands. As John C. Maxwell likes to say, "God's grip doesn't slip!" The key is to seek God and his forgiveness when you fall. God's grace is stronger than sin. You are not saved by your confession but by God's grace alone.

What if you do not make confession a regular part of your life? You will become hardened to sin, and you will sacrifice joy. As John Mac-Arthur writes, "I've seen Christians—judicially forgiven and eternally secure—who are hardened, impenitent, and insensitive to sin. Consequently, they are also without joy because they do not have a loving, intimate fellowship with God. They have blocked out joy and fellowship with the barricade of their unconfessed sin."[8]

Confession is a much better route!

Remember, though, that God's amazing grace does not grant you a license to sin. My youth pastor, Johnny Square, always said, "God's grace is nowhere to wipe your feet." Johnny meant that grace is not cheap and is not to be taken for granted. The Christian journey should be characterized by becoming more like Christ every day. Christians are not sinless but should have the desire to sin less through fellowship with him. As you confess your sins and walk in intimate fellowship with him, God will transform you.

HOW TO CONFESS

To be forgiven for your sins, you must confess them to God. Confession means agreeing with God that your actions or thoughts are contrary to his will. Confession takes his side, not your own. Confession means telling him how you have wronged him.

If a confessing prayer is new to you, consider applying several guidelines:

- *Be specific.* It is critical to "unpack" the specific sin—to go deeper than offering generalities. Tell God about the specific thought or action that was contrary to his character. When you confess your sins, call them out for what they are—lust, envy, greed, deceit, hatred, anger, or whatever is on your heart. Being specific demonstrates your responsibility. If you get mad and punch a hole in the wall in front of your spouse, do not simply say, "I sinned, please forgive me." You show greater recognition of your sin when you say, "I lost my temper, became angry, and punched a hole in the wall. I didn't exercise self-control and scared my wife. I was wrong. I'm sorry and I seek your forgivness."
- *Be sincere.* God requires a broken and contrite heart when we confess sin (Ps. 51:17). From the depths of your heart, sincerely acknowledge your wrongdoing. Sin by its very nature is harmful to our relationship with God and those around us. Being honest about the brokenness we have caused in our relationships and how we have hurt others helps us see the seriousness of our sin.
- *Seek forgiveness.* Ask God to forgive you for the wrong, cleansing you from all unrighteousness in the name of his Son, Jesus Christ. King David writes, "Create in me a clean heart, O God, and renew a right spirit within me" (Ps. 51:10). Ask God to do the same for you.
- *Believe.* Know that once you have confessed your sins, you are forgiven. Take God at his word. Again, read the wise words from King David: "I acknowledged my sin to you, and I did not cover my iniquity; I said, 'I will confess my transgressions to the LORD,' and you forgave the iniquity of my sin" (Ps. 32:5).
- *Move on.* Satan will try to make you feel ashamed and ineffective because of your sin. Once you have confessed your sin and have repented, let go of the guilt and move on. Trusting that God has forgiven and cleansed you, you must also forgive yourself.

- *Trust that God is working.* Once you confess your sins, God's trans-forming power continues to change your life. He will change your motives and desires as he reshapes you. Through the power of the Holy Spirit, he will move you in his direction.
- *Change your ways.* Repentance is the changing of your mind about your sin. You turn away from it, and you go another direction. You align yourself with God. It is your responsibility to remove the objects of sin from your life. Maybe you need to put down the bottle, stop watching that show, take a break from that friend group, stop scrolling on those social media feeds, knock down those idols of status and success, or throw away that magazine that tempts you. Identify the things that cause you trouble and remove them.
- *Build a habit.* Confession should be a daily exercise. Do not let a day pass where you have not confessed your sins to God and repented. Keep your accounts short with God. Do not let sins build up. Take care of them right away.

A confessing prayer that specifically and sincerely asks for and receives forgiveness, followed by a movement away from sin and a willingness to let God continue his work in and through you, will change you from the inside out. Making confession a habit will change you so deeply that God will change others through you.

When the Holy Spirit convicts you of sin and you confess it, you allow God to shed light on your darkened path. As you move toward the light, you will grow more sensitive to God's will and ways. As Lawrence Richards explains, "In the radiance of the light of Jesus, we become aware of pools of darkness in ourselves. Things we did that before seemed natural and proper become tawdry and shameful. Motives we suppressed come to light."[9]

You have an open door to confess your sins to God and seek his for-giveness. He will hear you, wipe away your sins, and restore your fel-lowship with him. Keeping short accounts with God will enable you to experience rich fellowship with the One who loves you, and being honest with God frees you to be honest with yourself and others.

INTEGRITY IN THE WORKPLACE

Discipled leaders are honest to the core and know that integrity is a foundational characteristic of successful leadership. Consider the last time you were faced with an ethical decision at your job that you knew you could get away with. Did you turn a blind eye to unmistakable wrongdoing? Did you feign ignorance to avoid responsibility? Did you play out different scenarios in your head to figure out which outcome would place you in the best position? Or did you choose to do the right thing regardless of the outcome—for others or for you?

Leaders face such decisions on a routine basis. Some companies are moral minefields. Some employees, coworkers, or bosses are ethical nightmares. To be discipled leaders with integrity, we must learn how to navigate the minefields and the nightmares without losing trust in ourselves, our teams, and our God. We must work hard to pursue truth no matter the cost. We must be leaders with integrity.

When you face a potentially unethical situation or behavior, I encourage you to do three things:

- *Stay true.* Integrity means remaining whole and sticking to a moral code or value. As discussed in chapter 1, regularly spending time in God's Word is the best way to learn wisdom, the difference between right and wrong on God's terms. Internalize what integrity means, then practice it privately and publicly. When you face a situation where you could fudge the numbers, shift the blame to someone else, or claim someone else's work as your own, stay true to doing what is right.
- *Build accountability.* A leader needs to develop personal and public controls—the ability to verify compliance to a set of standards. Be transparent about goals, methods, and shortfalls. Leaders must be willing to be held accountable and to hold others accountable. Putting appropriate controls in place will help prevent unethical or immoral behaviors. If such controls are not put in place, people will deviate from expectations and fall into corruption. The Bible says, "Righteousness guards the person of integrity, but wickedness overthrows the sinner" (Prov. 13:6 NIV). Remember that part

of effective accountability is creating an environment where mistakes and failures can be confessed safely, restoration is possible, and team members are supported when they move forward in learning from their mistakes.

- *Speak up.* If you see something wrong, say something—no matter the cost. Integrity requires courage but will make a positive difference in the long run. Go out of your way to create a team environment where others feel comfortable speaking up as well. Encourage honesty and constructive criticism, and make sure team members are not punished or bullied for calling out issues and mistakes.

You cannot will yourself to do the right thing at the right time all the time. Integrity flows from a heart and mind at peace with God.

Practice the principles of staying true, building accountability, and speaking up when faced with challenging circumstances and you will become a leader known for your integrity. Being a leader with integrity does not just happen. You cannot will yourself to do the right thing at the right time all the time. Integrity flows from a heart and mind at peace with God. In other words, you are able to do the right thing despite the consequences—even to yourself—because you ultimately trust God for the outcome. Establishing that trust through confession in your own life is essential to the Christian life.

THE REST OF THE STORY

Unfortunately, one more consequence resulted from uncovering the side-business hustle operation going on at work. The investigation revealed that Evan might have seen the signals but had turned a blind eye to them, so he was considered complicit and forced to retire.

It was a bittersweet moment. I had worked with the team for years and did not want any harm to come to them. At the same time, I knew I needed to expose the wrong I saw. For years after these displacements, I worked in fear of retribution, thinking that someone would take revenge for my standing up for what was right. Gratefully, that never happened.

Whenever I am tempted to skirt the truth in my words or actions, I think about that logo and side gig that ultimately cost multiple people their jobs. Leaders at the company had lied, both actively and by omission, and their dishonesty led to their removal from the company. It does not take much for a house of cards to fall.

It is essential for leaders to lead with integrity. If you are the one responsible for building a strong team or a strong company, your peers and employees need to know they can trust you.

THE PRICE OF HONESTY

Just as dishonesty can pull a division apart, honesty can heal a team that is struggling to function. Honesty can also be painful, but its huge rewards are worth it.

"Your team would like to hold a leadership assimilation next week," my manager said.

"Really? That's surprising. Why?" I asked.

"They feel like they aren't being heard," he replied.

I slumped in my chair. We were missing deadlines, experiencing quality issues, and suffering from infighting. This leadership role was nothing like I had imagined when I was promoted to manage the fifteen-person team.

As a matter of fact, I could feel something was wrong. I wrote in my journal just before hearing about the leadership assimilation, "I've gotten so far away from leading. I need to begin rethinking how I approach my team and begin to catalyze its transformation. How? I need to invest more time in connecting, building trust, capabilities, development, coaching, strategic thinking, rewarding, expressing appreciation, and listening. I've become more of an administrator and less of a leader. Less inspiring."

As I thought about what I had written and considered what type of feedback a "leadership assimilation" would produce, I was scared. Could

I take the stinging criticism? Would my team revolt? Was my job in jeopardy?

But I quickly concluded that if we needed a formal feedback session, I was open to it because I believed the session would accelerate my team's cohesiveness and provide clear feedback on my leadership style and blind spots. I was anxious about what I would hear, but I was also excited because it would enable us to improve.

I turned back to my manager. "I'll clear my schedule. Let me know when and where. I want to help solve any potential issues and address concerns."

Later that week, a human resources associate gathered the team together in a large conference room. The exercise was to address the question, "What do we need to become a high-performing team?" I told them I was open to their feedback and wanted to do whatever was necessary to improve. Then I left the room to allow the team to talk freely and went back to my office. They would call when they were ready.

One hour went by. Then two hours, then three hours. After four hours, they called me back into the room.

When I entered, many of them did not make eye contact. My blood pressure rose. I sat down silently and glanced at some bullet points they had written on a flip chart. The brave spokesperson outlined some of the group's thoughts:

- Preston isn't present during conversations—doesn't listen well and rushes through discussions.
- At the end of a conversation he always asks, "What can I do for you?" and comes across as inauthentic, like he asks but won't do anything.
- We need a leader who understands our work. "Be humble, don't be afraid to get your hands dirty."
- Too many fire drills, and we are experiencing inordinate amount of stress.
- Team doesn't feel like they can raise or explain concerns.
- Lack of recognition.

I will stop there. The team listed other issues, but you get the point.

It was a humbling experience, but the team was right. I had missed the leadership mark. Still, I was committed to listening to their concerns and changing things for the better.

At the end of the session, I looked around the room and admitted, "I am sorry. You deserve much stronger leadership. I accept responsibility and will work with you to make the changes you outlined. Will you help me?"

Smiles broke out across the conference table and the team responded with an emphatic "Yes."

That leadership assimilation was a turning point for me and for the team. I was able to lead by example with my willingness to listen, admit wrong, reward openness, and change my actions. The team collaboratively problem-solved, and we enacted their recommended solutions. I adjusted my approach. The team moved toward high performance.

When dealing with shortcomings in the workplace, whether they are yours or those of your team members, there are three things you can do that will go a long way toward repairing relationships and restoring team functionality.

- *Be humble.* Be willing to admit when when you are wrong. Take the position of a servant. Think less about yourself and your goals and more about how to help others. I had to shift my mindset and prepare myself for the feedback. If I had not, I would have lost the team.
- *Learn to listen.* Top leaders know that listening is a crucial part of communication. Learn to love listening and engaging in the stories of others. Try to really pay attention during a conversation instead of being distracted by your phone or other device. Have one conversation at a time to give each person your full attention. Be present. Practice retelling the person's story in your mind to get better at listening. Everyone wants to be heard. Others will notice that you are listening to them and will leave your conversations thinking what a great communicator you are when all you really did was

listen. After the leadership assimilation, I stopped everything when someone wanted to talk, and I devoted my attention to them.

- *Promote transparency.* Drive open, honest, two-way communication. Accept feedback as a gift. Be willing to challenge thinking and push the envelope. When faced with problems or conflict, talk things out, remembering to always focus on the issue at hand, not the person. I appreciated the team's courage to share their frustrations with me. We were able to make the necessary changes, and the team flourished.

Although honesty often comes with a cost to your pride, dishonesty comes at a greater cost to your integrity, your character, and your relationships. No one wants to follow a leader they can't trust. But if you are a leader who is honest—with others, with God, and with yourself—you can transform your team, your workplace, and the world around you.

As a disciple, keep short accounts with God.

As a leader, be honest to the core.

QUESTIONS

- Honesty is the top quality people desire in a leader. Why do you think it is so important to leadership?
- Have you ever been in a circumstance where your integrity was tested? How did you apply the principles of staying true, building accountability, and speaking up? What happened, and what did you learn?
- Have you ever been honest with someone and the relationship was broken? What were the consequences, and would you change anything?
- What happens if you try to conceal your sin?
- Are you reviewing your life throughout the day, confessing any known sin? Why or why not? How can you make confession a regular part of your day?
- How will these discipleship and leadership principles help you transform your workplace through your pursuit of Christ?

CHAPTER FIVE

TALK

As a disciple, pray without ceasing.

As a leader, keep calm in the storm.

Don't fret or worry. Instead of worrying, pray. Let petitions
and praises shape your worries into prayers, letting God know
your concerns. Before you know it, a sense of God's wholeness,
everything coming together for good, will come and settle you
down. It's wonderful what happens when Christ displaces worry
at the center of your life.

—PHILIPPIANS 4:6–7 MSG

MY NO-NONSENSE MANAGER surveyed the roomful of team leaders and commanded us, "Bring your three-year plans. Have them complete and on my desk in two weeks."

We were supposed to nod our heads in silent assent. But I had to say something. If I did not, I knew my team would suffer.

"Catherine, we have so many priorities, and the team is under a lot of pressure to deliver on time. Can we delay the planning for a few weeks and allow them to remain focused on work that matters?"

I think it was those last three words that made her face turn red. Noticeably agitated, she turned toward the other managers in the room, my peers, and asked, "Do any of *you* have the same concerns?"

When all she received were shaking heads, she went around the room and asked for verbal confirmation. Every manager said they would be able to deliver on her request.

I could not believe what I was hearing. In the days leading up to that meeting, every manager there had shared with me how much pressure they were under and how challenged they felt because of Catherine's demands. Yet there they were, throwing me under the bus.

Catherine turned to me. "There you have it. No one else has a concern, and neither should you. Just go fill out one of your priority grids and you'll figure it out." Her words dripped with sarcasm.

As I let the silence sit, my mind flashed back to a year earlier, when I had been reluctant even to take this position. During my interview, I had been warned, "In the world of racks and point-of-sale material, everyone has an opinion on the merchandising elements: design, construction, cost, and deployment. You'll have multiple masters and need to serve them all. It will be a tough role. Extremely stressful, demanding, and political." Fearing I didn't know what I was getting myself into, the interviewer asked, "Do you think you've got what it takes?"

Everything I knew about that division came to my mind: their team was dysfunctional, the supply chain was impotent, and, just as my interviewer had said, there were too many chiefs. Any measure of success appeared impossible.

"I have what it takes, but I'm not interested in the role. Could you remove my name from consideration?"

She nodded her head, but I could tell she was shocked by my reply.

In the coming days, other leaders kept suggesting I was the right fit. Some even hinted that for me to turn down this role could have future career implications. Hesitantly—and knowing what predicaments likely awaited me—I accepted the offer.

During my first year in the new position, each of my fears came true. The team was overworked. They had low morale from feeling undervalued. Our suppliers always seemed to miss project deadlines. Designs were not relevant. The procurement team had more control over our projects than our marketing team. Our internal key stakeholders, our customers, and our bottlers were not satisfied with my team's performance. Each offered suggestions for how we—I—could do things differently.

Our work environment was chaos. Extreme stress was the norm.

I felt anxious all the time, worrying every day about what would go wrong. When inevitable mistakes were made, I feared whiplash. I couldn't sleep. I stopped exercising regularly because I had no time for it. On the rare moments when I was home, I was distant and easily aggravated. I was running scared, running on empty, and ready to burn out. I never felt like I was making a difference—anywhere.

I told my manager that I felt like I was failing on a daily basis. She was unsympathetic. I don't know why I thought talking with her would help. She had seldom listened to my concerns before. If she had, I rarely saw the result. So her singling me out during that managers' meeting should not have surprised me.

Being called out in front of my peers was embarrassing. I was stunned and flustered. I had to make an immediate decision as to how I would respond. I did not want to give up, but something had to change. I needed to raise my team's morale. I needed to empower them. I needed to increase our productivity. I needed to become a better leader. Rather than choose discouragement, I needed to opt for perseverance.

If I could not accomplish those tasks, anyone on my team could be out of a job. And if I could not save my team—and complete my three-year plan—I would not be the one under the bus . . . I would be driving it at my next job.

THE NEGLECTED DUTY

That staff meeting was a turning point. Instead of sulking, complaining behind my manager's back, or quitting, I chose the route I should have chosen all along: I prayed. I asked for God's wisdom to navigate this professional storm. I turned the circumstance over to him and asked for his peace. I sought his supernatural strength and resilience to keep going.

Prayer is an essential spiritual discipline because it is an opportunity to connect with the living God.

I did not resort to prayer earlier in my troubles, likely for the same reasons that you don't. As leaders, we think we have most everything under control. Or, if our work environment is chaotic, we naively think that if we just put in a little more effort, we can turn the ship around. We do that until we burn out, give up, or quit.

Why don't we pray first and more often? R. C. Sproul writes, "Our trouble is that we don't understand that prayer is to the Christian what breath is to life, yet no duty of the Christian is so neglected."[1] Our default mode is to be self-reliant and not seek God. Often, we pray only when it is our last resort. But prayer is an essential spiritual discipline because it is an opportunity to connect with the living God.

Consider it this way: What if your employees or team members only came to you with a problem once they were *already* in way over their heads? Wouldn't that frustrate you, knowing that, with your knowledge and accrued expertise, you could have helped them avoid those pitfalls? And, because you care for them and your company, you *wanted* to help them—but they never thought to ask you because they thought you were too busy.

Maybe this is a little bit how God feels about our prayer lives. If only we knew how much he cares, how available he is, and how he longs to help us, we would not be so timid, so forgetful, or so lazy about approaching him. John MacArthur gets at this when he writes, "As our Heavenly Father, he longs for fellowship with us, and he wants to know what is on our hearts—our needs and concerns. [We] may become tired of listening to people, but God's ears are never satiated—He is never wearied by [our] prayers."[2]

Still, even if we believe in God's immense love, our prayer lives rarely show it. We do not go to him as often as we ought to. Or we get discouraged and decide prayer does not "work" because God does not answer our prayers the way that we want him to. I believe this is because we do not have a firm grasp on another essential aspect of God's character.

GLORY BE TO GOD

What is the goal of the Christian life? Why do we pray? The Westminster Shorter Catechism states that "man's chief end is to glorify God, and to enjoy him forever."[3] Simply put, our job is to bring honor and glory to God and enjoy our relationship with him throughout eternity.

Because *glory* is such a weighty word, I will gladly allow J. I. Packer to unpack the term for you:

> God's goal is his glory, but this needs careful explanation, for it is easily misunderstood. It points to a purpose not of divine egoism, as is sometimes imagined, but of divine love. Certainly, God wants to be praised for his praiseworthiness and exalted for his greatness and goodness; he wants to be appreciated for

what he is. . . . "Glory" in the Old Testament carries associations of weight, worth, wealth, splendor, and dignity, all of which are present when God is said to have revealed his glory. . . . New Testament writers proclaim that the glory of God's nature, character, power, and purpose is now open to view in the person and role of God's incarnate Son, Jesus Christ.[4]

God wants to reveal his glory—who he is, in all the fullness of his love, grace, and power—to his people. God's glory is revealed in his Son and his plan of salvation; this alone merits our praise. We also glorify God by honoring him in our everyday lives. God is jealous for his glory. He is the sole giver and sustainer of life. No one else contributed to his works of creation or salvation. No one loves us like he does. He is the only God. Our role is to glorify God—to point to what he has done, give him the credit, and bring honor to his name.

This is important to understand because God answers prayers that glorify *his* name and are for *your* benefit. God does not always answer our prayers exactly the way we want. God is completely faithful, so he will act according to his character, revealing who he is and his glory, and doing what is best for us, even if we cannot understand it at the time.

It is your job to examine your heart. What are your attitudes and motives? Are you seeking God for a comfortable life, or are you seeking him to bring glory to his name? Are your desires *his* desires? If you are walking in intimate fellowship with the Lord, the Holy Spirit will move you to pray for what glorifies him.

Ultimately, your desire to pray reflects the condition of your heart.

HOW TO PRAY

God is calling you to be a person of prayer. The Bible says, "The prayer of a righteous person is powerful and effective" (James 5:16 NIV). If you seek God in prayer, he moves mountains, transforms lives, and changes circumstances. You must have faith that God loves you and wants the very best for you.

You should also desire great things from God and not settle for less. By great things I do not mean notoriety, a hefty balance sheet, or the top of the corporate ladder. I am talking about walking with God, experiencing his joy, and being filled with his peace. As C. S. Lewis famously writes,

> If we consider the unblushing promises of reward and the staggering nature of the rewards promised in the Gospels, it would seem that Our Lord finds our desires not too strong, but too weak. We are half-hearted creatures, fooling about with drink and sex and ambition when infinite joy is offered us, like an ignorant child who wants to go on making mud pies in a slum because he cannot imagine what is meant by the offer of a holiday at the sea. We are far too easily pleased.[5]

If this is the case and prayer does make a difference, learning to pray and prioritizing prayer ought to be essential for every discipled leader. As Warren Wiesbe encourages, "[Prayer] is our opportunity to approach God and express our hearts. Prayer is the highest and deepest expression of the inner person."[6] Your "heart" includes your mind, will, and emotions all wrapped up into one. The heart is your deepest inner being.

If your heart is faithful, humble, and reverent, God will fill you with an all-consuming fire for him.

As you approach God, remember these three heart postures:

- *Faithfulness.* As God's children, we should be confident that God is in complete control and wants what is best for us. The Bible says, "We know that for those who love God all things work together for good, for those who are called according to his purpose" (Rom. 8:28). That's faith—trusting God. Your faith in God and his promises is the starting point of communicating with him. And you must be faithful in prayer, just as Jesus was. As Wiersbe reminds us, "Our Lord lived by faith and depended on prayer during his life and ministry on earth. Now if Jesus Christ, with all his power and perfection, had to depend on prayer, how much more do you and I, with our multiplied imperfections and weaknesses, need to depend on prayer!"[7]

- *Humility.* Leaders tend to be self-confident and self-reliant, thinking they can do everything on their own. Humility believes the opposite. Being humble is to realize that you depend on God for everything. When you pray, do not be self-centered.
- *Reverence.* God is holy, and it is our duty to respect and honor him. When you pray, you are in God Almighty's presence. You are only able to do this because of Jesus's death on the cross for your sins, the substitution of his life for yours. It is an absolute privilege to approach God with your needs and concerns. You must also understand that God is not at your beck and call, like a genie, whenever you get into a jam or need something. Do not treat him flippantly. Out of respect for who he is, approach him reverently.

If your heart is faithful, humble, and reverent, God will fill you with an all-consuming fire for him. You will develop a thirst for God as you spend time alone with him in prayer.

If your heart is right before God, how then do you pray? Jesus provided a model prayer for us in Matthew 6:9–13, what we call the Lord's Prayer. I appreciate the way *The Message* paraphrases it in today's language: "Our Father in heaven, reveal who you are. Set the world right; do what's best—as above, so below. Keep us alive with three square meals. Keep us forgiven with you and forgiving others. Keep us safe from ourselves and the Devil. You're in charge! You can do anything you want! You're ablaze in beauty! Yes. Yes. Yes."

The Lord's Prayer is the definitive structure for communicating with God. Jesus points us to addressing God as our Father, glorifying his name, asking that his will be done and that God's kingdom be visible on earth just as it is in heaven, and requesting provision, forgiveness, and protection.

Using the Lord's Prayer as the example, consider these four main components of prayer: adoration, confession, thanksgiving, and supplication (ACTS).[8] These components are not a method for prayer but rather a simple framework to follow as you connect with God.

- *Adoration.* Begin your prayers by praising and honoring God. Worship sets the tone for time alone with God. Praise pleases him when it comes from a loving and surrendered heart. Your challenge may be that you often do not know how to articulate God's greatness, or you may not know much about him. The solution is to become very familiar with Scripture, like the book of Psalms, which is filled with magnificent expressions about God and his holiness. Scripture will help move you from stammering to significant adoration.
- *Confession.* In the practice of keeping short accounts with God, confess your sins. We discussed confession in depth in the previous chapter, but it is worth repeating that you should regularly seek God's forgiveness and ask him to wash you as white as snow. Remember, the Bible says, "If we confess our sins, he is faithful and just to forgive us our sins and to cleanse us from all unrighteousness" (1 John 1:9). It is best to deal with your sins before you address God with requests. In confession, you unpack your specific sins and humbly seek his forgiveness.
- *Thanksgiving.* This may well be one of the most forgotten components of prayer. We simply do not thank God for all that he has done in our lives or for the prayers he has answered. You might have an "attitude of gratitude," a feeling of thanks, but thanksgiving is different because it is gratitude expressed. As Christians, we must remember that we have "passed from death to life; from alienation to acceptance; from despair to hope; from danger to safety; from uncertainty to peace."[9] If you grasp who God is and what he has done, thanksgiving will naturally play a prominent part in your prayers.
- *Supplication.* This is making your requests known to God, approaching his throne with a humble heart, boldness, and confidence, ex-

pressing your needs or concerns. Supplication is your opportunity to seek God's intervention and have faith that he will answer in his perfect timing and according to his perfect will. If your prayers are in alignment with God's will, he will do great things to glorify his name and move on your behalf.

Following the ACTS framework can help you establish and maintain a robust prayer life. But you can also build upon that framework. The Bible provides additional insight about how to pray effectively.

- *Let the Holy Spirit guide you.* The Holy Spirit initiates and inspires your prayers. "Likewise the Spirit helps us in our weakness. For we do not know what to pray for as we ought, but the Spirit himself intercedes for us with groanings too deep for words" (Rom. 8:26). With this incredible help, you can be fully confident when approaching God with requests.
- *Work toward frequency.* Prayer should become a lifestyle for all believers. As Paul encourages, "Pray without ceasing" (1 Thess. 5:17). Take every moment and opportunity to pray. Make it a continual conversation with God and a way of life.
- *Persevere.* Your prayers should be full of passion and persistence. Jesus wants us to pray and not become discouraged with delays. In Luke 18:1–8, Jesus tells a story about a widow whose persistent request for justice compels a judge to render such justice after initially refusing. Continually bothered by the widow, the judge ruled "so that she will not beat me down by her continual coming" (Luke 18:5). As John MacArthur writes, "If you don't get an immediate answer to your request, or if events don't turn out exactly or as quickly as you hoped they would, our Lord's word to us is 'don't lose heart.' Just keep praying without ceasing and don't give up. Keep knocking. Keep asking. Keep seeking."[10]
- *Have confidence.* Approach God with the assurance that he is your Father and he listens to you. The Bible encourages us to "walk right up to God, into 'the Holy Place.' Jesus has cleared the way by the blood of his sacrifice, acting as our priest before God. The 'curtain'

into God's presence is his body. So, let's do it—full of belief, confident that we're presentable inside and out. Let's keep a firm grip on the promises that keep us going. He always keeps his word" (Heb. 10:19–23 MSG). Because Jesus "cleared the way" and God loves you, approach him with confidence.

- *Pray in secret.* When you pray, God wants you to do it in private and not draw attention to yourself. Jesus says, "Here's what I want you to do: Find a quiet, secluded place so you won't be tempted to role-play before God. Just be there as simply and honestly as you can manage. The focus will shift from you to God, and you will begin to sense his grace" (Matt. 6:6 MSG). If you do pray in public, pray as you would if you were in private. Do not try to impress anyone with big words or dramatic prayers.

- *Be concise.* God does not require long, drawn-out prayers or chanting to get his attention. Jesus taught his disciples to be succinct: "And when you pray, do not keep on babbling like pagans, for they think they will be heard because of their many words. Do not be like them, for your Father knows what you need before you ask him" (Matt. 6:7–8 NIV). Focus on the substance of your prayers, being mindful and straight to the point.

- *Pray "in Jesus's name."* The Bible instructs us to pray in the name of Jesus (John 16:23). Why? Jesus's name reflects who he is and his character—he's the go-between for us and God (Heb. 4:14–16). Pray confidently in Jesus's name because of who he is.

- *Say "Amen."* Why do we end our prayers this way? *Amen* means "so be it." Saying "amen" affirms that the prayer is true and that you are aligned with it.

NINE SUGGESTED PRAYER TOPICS

If you are unsure of what or whom to pray for, the following suggestions can guide you in developing the habit of prayer. As you make your requests to God, look beyond your circumstances and needs. God wants to help you, but he also wants to accomplish his will in and through you.

- *Your heart's desires.* John MacArthur puts it this way: "God wants to give you the desire of your heart as long as your desire is consistent with his."[11] Psalm 145:16 states, "You open your hand; you satisfy the desire of every living thing." God is kind and generous. He wants to know what's on your heart and to meet your needs.
- *Kingdom expansion.* Pray for God's will to be done on earth as it is in heaven—that the invisible becomes visible. Pray that the gospel—the good news that Jesus Christ died for our sins and rose again—is shared, that people surrender their lives to Jesus, and that they grow spiritually. Pray that God's promises are fulfilled. Pray that you are effective and productive as you walk with him.
- *Fellow believers.* Pray for other Christians as if they were members of your family. We are all interconnected through our relationship with God. The Bible says, "If one member suffers, all suffer together; if one member is honored, all rejoice together" (1 Cor. 12:26). Pray for their victory over sin, protection, provision, and growth in their walk with Christ. If they are successful, the church is successful. If they fail, it impacts the church in a negative way.
- *The lost.* We must have a passion and zeal for others to come to Christ. As MacArthur notes, "The central function of the Church on earth is to reach the lost."[12] Paul writes in his letter to the Roman Christians, "Brothers, my heart's desire and prayer to God for them is that they may be saved" (Rom. 10:1). Do you know someone who does not know Jesus? Pray for them and watch God work.
- *Protection.* As we will discuss more fully in the next chapter, you are in a spiritual battle, and our enemy wants nothing more than to destroy you. He hates us because he hates God. Pray for protection from "the enemy who would destroy the work of Christ in this world."[13] But take courage: the Bible also says, "If God is for us, who can be against us?" (Rom. 8:31). God is all-powerful, loves you, and will protect you.
- *Wisdom.* Ask God for the ability to discern right from wrong, for insight into how to handle problems, and for discretion in dealing with people. Proverbs is an incredible book when you are seeking wisdom. It says that wisdom is more valuable than gold (Prov.

8:10–11). It will keep you from stumbling on your Christian journey. It will deliver you from foolish and evil ways. Proverbs 3:5–6 says, "Trust GOD from the bottom of your heart; don't try to figure out everything on your own. Listen for GOD's voice in everything you do, everywhere you go; he's the one who will keep you on track. Don't assume that you know it all" (MSG). Ask God for wisdom and he will give it freely (James 1:5).

- *Worthiness.* Pray that you will please God in your walk with him. Colossians 1:9–10 says, "We have not ceased to pray for you, asking that you may be filled with the knowledge of his will in all spiritual wisdom and understanding, so as to *walk in a manner worthy of the Lord*, fully pleasing to him: bearing fruit in every good work and increasing in the knowledge of God" (emphasis added). What are the characteristics of a worthy walk? Humility, purity, contentment, faith, righteousness, unity, gentleness, patience, love, joy, thankfulness, knowledge, wisdom, truth, and fruitfulness. As John the apostle writes, "Whoever says he abides in him ought to walk in the same way in which he walked" (1 John 2:6). Pray that you may please God and be worthy of him.

- *Faithfulness.* Paul prayed for the strength of believers and their faithfulness: "We pray that you'll have the strength to stick it out over the long haul—not the grim strength of gritting your teeth but the glory-strength God gives. It is strength that endures the unendurable and spills over into joy, thanking the Father who makes us strong enough to take part in everything bright and beautiful that he has for us" (Col. 1:11–12 MSG). Pray for God's strength and to be found faithful in your Christian journey.

- *Government leaders.* Our civic leaders need great wisdom in dealing with our many domestic and international challenges. Paul encouraged his disciple Timothy to pray for their leaders: "First of all, then, I urge that supplications, prayers, intercessions, and thanksgivings be made for all people, for kings and all who are in high positions, that we may lead a peaceful and quiet life, godly and dignified in every way" (1 Tim. 2:1–2). Remember to pray for your leaders!

While the above list is in no way all-inclusive, it is a great start. God also commands us to pray for our enemies, for the healing of our country, and for revival. If we realize that we are part of something much greater than ourselves and that we can influence God through our prayers, we ought to engage him on many fronts.

HINDRANCES TO PRAYER

What if you pray and feel as if nothing happens, as if your prayers don't go beyond the ceiling? Fortunately, how we feel about our prayers does not determine whether God hears us or is answering our prayers. However, your prayer life may be hindered or ineffective for many reasons.

- *Pride.* John MacArthur rightly observes, "No sin is more powerful or destructive than pride."[14] It's putting yourself before God. Pride believes you do not really need God's help. R. C. Sproul writes, "One of the things that betrays our fallen condition is the concept of the self-made man, one who takes credit for the bounty of his goods and forgets the source of all his provision. We must remember that God gives us all we have in the ultimate sense."[15] When we are filled with pride, our prayer life will be hindered because we will not fully trust God with our circumstances. We will think we can handle life's challenges on our own and will not share our requests humbly and reverently with God.
- *Ingratitude.* This is the opposite of appreciation. Ingratitude forgets God and what he has done in your life. In Luke 17, Jesus went out of his way to heal ten lepers. While all ten were healed and probably grateful for the healing, only one returned to actually thank him. The other nine did not stop to fully appreciate God's strength and care. Remember to thank God. Do not allow your heart to be hardened by ingratitude. Remembering God's daily provision will remind you to come to him again and again with your prayers.
- *Unresolved conflicts.* Your relationships with others matter to God. If there is tension, bitterness, hatred, anger, or resentment between

you and someone else, it is up to you to seek resolution and forgive others before approaching God. Jesus says, "This is how I want
you to conduct yourself in these matters. If you enter your place
of worship and, about to make an offering, you suddenly remember a grudge a friend has against you, abandon your offering, leave
immediately, go to this friend and make things right. Then and
only then, come back and work things out with God" (Matt. 5:23–
24 MSG). It insults God when you withhold forgiveness and grace
from those who ask it of you while you claim to be forgiven and
saved by grace yourself. Remember that "forgiven people forgive
other people."[16] So, before you seek God in prayer, resolve your out-
standing conflicts.

- *Marital discord.* If you are married, God takes notice of how you
  treat your spouse. If there are arguments and friction between
  married couples, that conflict interrupts the relationship and
  produces separation. Treating your spouse with honor and dignity and loving them the way Christ loved the church produces
  unity. The Bible says, "Husbands, in the same way be considerate as you live with your wives, and treat them with respect as
  the weaker partner and as heirs with you of the gracious gift of
  life, so that nothing will hinder your prayers" (1 Peter 3:7 NIV).
  Marital discord will also interrupt and impede your prayers. We
  cannot say that we love God and yet hate our spouse (1 John 4:20).
  Determine to treat your spouse well and your prayer life will not
  be hindered.

- *Unrepentance.* If you are living an unrepentant life, harboring sin
  in your heart—rationalizing it, indulging in it, treasuring it, even
  delighting in it—God will not hear your prayers. The Bible says, "If
  I had cherished iniquity in my heart, the Lord would not have listened" (Ps. 66:18).

The bottom line is that sin hinders your prayer life. It can be sin
against God or sin against others. A key part of your walk with God is
realizing that sin obstructs your interaction with him and that honest confession—bringing to God your shame, your tendency to hide and

blame, and your repentance—will open the lines of communication with him.

> *The life of a Christian walking with God is marked by peace, and this "peace that passes all understanding" will allow you to navigate the inevitable storms of leading others.*

When your communication with God is free and consistent, you can't help but notice the spiritual growth taking place in you. As you nurture your prayer life, that spiritual growth will naturally find its way into your daily life. Consequently, knowing how to pray—and actually praying—will make you a better leader. Why? Because the life of a Christian walking with God is marked by peace, and this "peace that passes all understanding" will allow you to navigate the inevitable storms of leading others.

"HIS CARE IS SUFFICIENT"

As a leader, keep calm in the storm.

Due to the immense burdens placed on leaders, we sometimes allow circumstances to drain our joy and peace. The domino effect begins: worry leads to anxiety, and anxiety leads to stress. Worry happens when you are consumed by nagging thoughts, self-doubt, uncertainties, fear of the unknown, or a potential threat. This all leads to anxiety—behavioral responses such as sweating, nervousness, and an increased heart rate. This leads to stress: the negative effect of sustained mental and physical pressure.

Sound familiar?

Fortunately, there is a way out. The disciplined leader does not need to be filled with anxiety. Roger Ellsworth reminds us, "Rather, we are to bring our problems and needs to the Lord with the confidence that he cares for us and his care is sufficient."[17] This does not mean our problems will suddenly resolve, however. As Warren Wiersbe explains, "Peace is the inner tranquility and confidence that God is in control. This does not mean the absence of trials on the outside, but it does mean a quiet confidence within, regardless of circumstances, people, or things."[18]

Worry, anxiety, and stress can be overcome by trusting God and turning everything over to him in prayer. As you rely on him and his grace, God will fill you with his peace and enable you to persevere through any storm.

If you face chaos, a dysfunctional team, and insurmountable odds, begin praying in these areas:

- *Gaining a clear focus.* If you or your team do not know what you want, you will not get it. If you do not know where you are going, any road will get you there. The Bible says, "Where there is no vision . . . the people perish" (Prov. 29:18 AMPC). Pray for a vision for your team and your organization's future. As a team, who do you want to be, where do you want to go, and what do you want to accomplish? A clear vision serves as a road map. Employees can easily ask themselves if their actions are contributing to the attainment of your vision. If the vision is a mist in your mind, it will be a fog in your team's minds. So know your focus and communicate it effectively.
- *Creating an engaged culture.* High-performing organizations typically have one thing in common: a highly engaged team. Engagement refers to the level of emotional connection associates have to their manager, team, and work environment. The stronger the emotional connection, the higher the performance—and vice versa. Disengaged associates can be a drag on performance. Pray that associates trust one another, feel safe, enjoy what they do, and have positive relationships with their managers and peers.
- *Prioritizing the priorities.* Not all things can be important. When you are feeling overwhelmed by deadlines and to-do lists, pray for God's peace and wisdom to help you cut through the chaos, prioritize the tasks at hand, and rank what needs to be done. Then, pray

for clarity and collaboration as you and your team focus all your energy on accomplishing the top priorities and moving to the next ones. As you implement this process, you will become more productive and efficient, and less stressed and distracted.

- *Empowering the team.* People are more committed to working if they know they can make decisions and have an impact on projects. They will help you accomplish common goals and objectives with vigor. Pray for God's leading as you identify (or review) the strengths of team members, delegate appropriate tasks, and strategize pathways for optimum workflow. Ask God for patience to listen to your team's feedback, and ask for his watchfulness as you oversee many moving parts. As you empower your team, you will reduce anxiety because people will feel like they have more control and can take ownership. If you do not empower your team, they will perceive their lack of influence and become detached. Pray for their motivation, connection, and ownership over the work.

- *Expanding your capacity.* Realize that pressure-filled situations enable you to grow and prepare you for the next opportunity. That is why making time for prayer—as well as exercise and adequate sleep—puts these situations in perspective and allows you to lean into them. Let the challenges stretch you. Thank God for the challenging opportunities he has put before you, and listen when he reminds you that he is faithful to complete the good work he started in you (Phil. 1:6). In one of my favorite Bible verses, God tells Jeremiah, "If you're worn out in this footrace with men, what makes you think you can race against horses? And if you can't keep your wits during times of calm, what's going to happen when troubles break loose like the Jordan in flood?" (Jer. 12:5 MSG). The verse reminds me that all of my experiences are preparing me for the next ones, building my capacity to handle them.

- *Expressing appreciation.* People need to know that their work matters and is valued and appreciated. Recognize their efforts, publicly and privately. Celebrate small wins to help build momentum toward big wins. Pray that you and your team will openly and frequently thank each other when a job is well done.

With God's leading through prayer, you will gain focus, create engagement, prioritize, empower your team, allow challenges to expand your capacity, and express appreciation. Then you will become a persevering leader, able to withstand any storm—or bus.

WHAT CHANGED MY TEAM AND ME

After that demoralizing meeting where my manager did not take me or my team's needs seriously, I began praying about my team's challenges on a regular basis. Through these times of prayer and communion with the God of all wisdom and grace, I was able to work from a place of peace instead of a place of fear and anxiety. I developed a vision of becoming our key stakeholders' most valuable partner and winning industry recognition. Then, asking for God's guidance, I identified significant projects that would influence the company's performance. With these priorities in place, I intentionally began building confidence in my employees. I knew that if I believed in them, they would believe in themselves. I empowered the team to make decisions and enabled them to say no to irrelevant, unproductive work.

The team began to gel and became more productive. They remained focused on priorities and ignored distractions. Their morale improved, and their stress levels lessened. So did mine. Our internal and external customers moved from doubting our ability to trusting us to deliver. Together, we made a lot of progress. The tables were turning.

Nowhere was this more evident than during my annual review. Though my manager used few words, the words she used mattered greatly to me. She simply said, "You are a difference-maker, and thank you for all of your hard work." Her affirmation was gratifying and validating. My team members received the highest annual rating: "exceeds performance," which, for our team, was unprecedented.

Looking back, I am so thankful for the experience, even having the bus driven over me. I came to know God's peace as I leaned on him for help. Through all the stress, emotions, and obstacles, I learned and grew more than I imagined. I was stretched to the limit and increased my work capacity beyond what I thought was possible. In that, too, I could pray to God in thankfulness and gratitude. With his help, I stayed true to my original goals, persevered with the team, and helped transform the business.

All because I made the simple choice to ask God for help.

QUESTIONS

- Do you trust God and believe that he is in control? Why or why not?
- Are you experiencing God's peace, or are you struggling with anxiety? If the latter, how is anxiety holding you back and limiting your prayers?
- Why is prayer important in a leader's life?
- What role does perseverance play in leadership, and why is it important? When is the last time you persevered and it paid off? What did you learn?
- How will these discipleship and leadership principles help you transform your workplace through your pursuit of Christ?

CHAPTER SIX

FLEE

As a disciple, resist the devil and he will flee.

As a leader, ask, "Is it worth it?"

No temptation has overtaken you that is not common to man. God is faithful, and he will not let you be tempted beyond your ability, but with the temptation he will also provide the way of escape, that you may be able to endure it.

—1 CORINTHIANS 10:13

FIVE HUNDRED MANAGERS and frontline associates sat on the other end of the conference call. I had just finished my fifteen-minute presentation explaining what we needed to do over the coming months. I thought my ideas had been insightful, clear, and to-the-point—maybe even inspiring.

I asked, "Any questions?"

I heard crickets.

Actually, I didn't hear anything. It did not take long for that silence to turn into a sinking feeling. Something was wrong. The presentation had gone well—I had prepared all week for it, after all—but not one person out of five hundred replied. I don't know if that had ever happened to me on a conference call before.

"Thank you all for your time. Goodbye." I hung up, mentally distraught and distressed. *What just happened?*

Just as that thought crossed my mind, my phone rang. I picked it up, grimacing in anticipation of the dressing-down that was sure to follow.

"Hi, Preston." My manager's voice was casual, but not as casual as normal.

"Hi, Don! What's up?" I tried to sound energetic. I'm not sure which one of us was the better bluffer. Likely neither.

"Just checking in. How did you think the call went today?"

"I feel like it went OK. I prepared all week and thought I hit all the key points. But I was a little concerned because no one asked questions like they normally do."

Don paused. "Can I give you some feedback?"

There it was: the reason for the call. "Sure, Don. Of course." I gripped the armrests of my office chair, physically bracing myself for his reply.

"You sounded way overprepared, plastic, and too scripted. You didn't come across well. I know you're well trained in public speaking, but today's presentation didn't connect. I recommend you adjust your approach next time and be more conversational. What do you think?"

Are you kidding me? Too overprepared? Isn't that what we do here? Isn't most of our time as managers spent preparing? And who are you, Don, to tell me how to present? I have all the training and experience! You just have a better office than me! What do you know about connecting with five hundred managers at once?

I strangled the armrests trying to find the right words for the moment. To his credit, Don waited for my reply. He likely knew I did not want to hear what he was saying.

"Thanks for the feedback, Don. I will consider how to improve my style before the next call."

"Thanks, Preston. I know you will."

We hung up, but I did not hang up my anger. I sat stewing in my office for the next few hours. I was tempted to call Don and strike back with the full fury of a well-trained *conversationalist.* Resentment rose. I wanted to tell him exactly what I thought of him. I wanted to say how much I *did not* appreciate his criticism. I wanted to shift blame to everything and everyone else—a tech problem with the call, or that I had done such an amazing job that no one had questions because I had so thoroughly covered everything. I was not bad at my job; I was *too good* at it.

I was so angry and proud and hurt that the temptation to save face was consuming me.

To say I was fuming would be putting it mildly.

I picked up my phone at least a dozen times, and I slammed it back down every time.

DEFINING TEMPTATION

There are only a few sure things in life: death, taxes, change, and *temptation.* Obviously, I have been tempted and not just in my interaction with Don but in every area of my life. I am willing to bet you have too. Temptation happens to everyone, anytime, anywhere.

You know what temptation is even if you have never read a clear definition of it—but I like definitions. Lawrence Richards defines tempta-tion as "a difficult situation, a pressure that brings a reaction through which the character or commitment of a believer is demonstrated."[1] Temptation is the enticement to sin.

Note that temptation *isn't* sinful. That's critical to know. Temptation becomes sin only when a suggested evil is yielded to and accepted.[2] There is a tipping point where you move from temptation into sin, a moment when you decide to sin. Christian author and speaker Richard Exley writes, "When a desire is born in us, we have a choice. . . . We can carefully refuse its existence altogether, since it needs our complicity to exist. Or else we can attend to it, think about it, fantasize it into greater existence—feed it! But if we do the latter, if we give it attention in our souls, soon we will be giving our souls to it. We've lost free will and the opportunity to choose. The desire itself overpowers us, commanding action, demanding satisfaction."[3]

How's that for a definition of what you *don't* want taking over your life?

When temptation births sin, sin births death—both physical and spiritual (James 1:15). It moves your heart away from God and out of fellowship with him until you seek his forgiveness. Remember as you read the rest of this chapter: temptation is not sinful; giving in to it is.

THE ORIGINS OF TEMPTATION

Temptation arises from three areas: the flesh, the devil, and the world. You may often find yourself simultaneously fighting battles on all three fronts.

The Flesh

When you became a Christian, you entered into a personal relationship with Jesus Christ. He made you a new creature and gave you a new heart. But your "flesh" remained—the sin nature you inherited when you were born. It is the part of you driven by the desire James speaks of when he says, "Each person is tempted when he is lured and enticed by his own desire" (James 1:14). These sinful desires are "against the Spirit, and the desires of the Spirit are against the flesh" (Gal. 5:17), and this opposition creates a constant inner conflict in you to obey God or rebel against him. The flesh distracts you from doing God's will.

The Devil

Satan and his army are the enemies of our souls. Satan "is 'the constant enemy of God, of Christ, of the divine kingdom, of the followers of Christ, and of all truth; full of falsehood and all malice, and exciting and seducing to evil in every possible way.' His power is very great in the world."[4]

The devil is your adversary and accuser. He wants to stop your worship of God and cut off your fellowship and communication with God. He manipulates your circumstances, exploits your weaknesses, creates doubt, makes you think you do not need God, sucks you in with temptation, laughs at you when you sin, and then accuses you for sinning.

The devil baits his hook with what we find the hardest to resist, appealing to both our flesh and spirit.

The Bible calls the devil our enemy, who "roams around like a lion roaring [in fierce hunger], seeking someone to seize upon and devour" (1 Peter 5:8 AMPC). The good news is that Satan is a limited being: he is not all-powerful, he is not all-knowing, and he cannot be everywhere at one time like God. He fears God and the blood of Christ in our lives.

But we must never underestimate Satan. The devil baits his hook with what we find the hardest to resist, appealing to both our flesh and spirit. When he baits us with a fleshly temptation, if we do not bite the bait, he changes to a spiritual lure such as pride, prejudice, or censorious criticism.[5] His aim is always to steal, kill, and destroy our fellowship with God.

The World

Sin reigns in the arena of "the world," a shorthand way of referring to the totality of humanity in the bondage of sin.[6] The world is the culture and conventional thought of society. It includes commonly accepted attitudes, preferences, and behaviors that people see as right in their own eyes but are against God's Word.

Through the media, Hollywood, and politics, Christians face the temptation to conform to the world's way of thinking. The apostle Paul warned the Romans, "Don't become so well-adjusted to your culture that you fit into it without even thinking. Instead, fix your attention on God. You'll be changed from the inside out. Readily recognize what he wants from you, and quickly respond to it. Unlike the culture around you, always dragging you down to its level of immaturity, God brings the best out of you, develops well-formed maturity in you" (Rom. 12:2 MSG).

Even though the flesh, the devil, and the world accost all of us, we are not all tempted by the same things. We may be enticed by pride, pleasure, money, power, lust, worldly glory, materialism, image, greed, sexual sin, laziness, bitterness, anger, envy, gluttony, drinking, drugs, stealing, or lying. Or we might be tempted *not* to do the right thing when we know we should, like going to church, tithing, sharing the gospel, reading the Bible, caring for our neighbors, feeding widows and orphans, providing for our families, raising up our children in the faith, or praying.

Why is that? Why are we tempted by such varied temptations? Because we are all wired differently from each other. In his famous devotional, *My Utmost for His Highest*, Oswald Chambers writes, "A man's disposition on the inside, i.e., what he possesses in his personality, determines what he is tempted by on the outside. The temptation fits the nature of the one tempted, and reveals the possibilities of the nature. Every man has the setting of his own temptation, and the temptation will come along the line of the ruling disposition."[7] In other words, my pride sets me up to be tempted to give my boss a piece of my mind when I do not agree with his well-meaning feedback about conference calls.

WHY WE ARE TRIED AND TEMPTED

Do you know how metals are prepared to be used in products? Steel, iron, and copper all go through a "smelting" process before they are ready for production. In the smelting process, the material ore is heated in a furnace until it liquifies. Impurities are separated from the liquid and thrown away. What is left is a pure liquid that is then cooled and molded to the producer's intent. Transforming material ore through the smelting process creates metal for things that are all around us: buildings, planes, cars, electronics, forks, knives, and so on.

You are ore in the smelting process.

> *God brings trials and allows temptations in your life*
> *to separate the pure from the impure.*

God brings trials and allows temptations in your life to separate the pure from the impure (Heb. 12:6–11). He puts you in situations that reveal your true character (i.e., integrity), show your devotion to him, and help your faith grow.

As Christians, we need to learn to distinguish between trials and temptations: "Temptations come from our desires within us (James 1:12–16) while trials come from the Lord who has a special purpose to fulfill. Temptations are used by the Devil to bring out the worst in us, but trials are used by the Holy Spirit to bring out the best in us (James 1:1–6)."[8] God does not tempt you (James 1:13), but he allows temptation in your life as part of the smelting process. God uses all things—even hardships and temptations—for the good of those who love him (Rom. 8:28). Over the course of your lifetime, God molds you into Christ's likeness.

But it sure doesn't feel like it at the moment, does it? When you are as angry as you have ever been and all you want to do is hit a wall—or worse? When you are lonely and all you want to do is watch what you would be ashamed to admit you watched? When you are fed up with your kids, spouse, parents, or employees for not listening to you and all you want to do is belittle them in your mind? When you are tempted to sin, it does not feel like a test. It just feels like life is hard. Your emotions are high (or low), and you can only see one outcome: an action you will likely regret in the near future.

But what if you chose to see such moments as tests of your faith?

What if you rewrote that "inevitable conclusion" to be something far more helpful?

A TALE OF TWO TEMPTED LEADERS

You likely already know your weak spots. You can probably name the temptations that have vexed you only recently and those that have taken up residency in your life. Unfortunately, experiencing temptation results from being human in a fallen world. You cannot escape temptation this side of heaven, but you can flee from it.

That is what discipled leaders do.

The biblical stories of King David and Joseph provide stellar examples. One shows what *not* to do when faced with temptation while the other shows what *to* do. David was the great and wealthy warrior king of Israel who lusted after another man's wife, Bathsheba (2 Sam. 11–12). He slept with her and fathered a son. To cover up his sin, he used his royal power to bring about the death of Bathsheba's husband, Uriah. In contrast, Joseph, the son of Jacob best known for his "coat of many colors," caught the attention of an Egyptian official's wife, who lusted after him (Gen. 39). Eventually, she grabbed for him but only tore his clothing because Joseph literally fled the scene. He was loyal both to God and to the woman's husband.

David and Joseph faced difficult circumstances and responded very differently. David allowed his temptation to lead him into sin, and that sin begot more sin. His lust led to adultery, and his adultery led to murder. He failed to flee the balcony from which he first saw Bathsheba, and he paid a high price for the sins that resulted. Eventually his children by multiple wives forged bitter rivalries that led to rape, incest, murder, and a bloody civil war. Yet David was not beyond forgiveness. He sought God's forgiveness, and God restored him. He was still "a man after [God's] own heart" (Acts 13:22 NIV).

In contrast, Joseph's right action—literally fleeing from temptation—resulted in a series of unjust events. The woman who had grabbed and torn his clothes used the torn piece to claim that Joseph had pursued *her* and forced himself upon her. Her false claims led her powerful husband to throw Joseph in jail. Yet Joseph remained faithful to God, was eventually released from prison, and subsequently rose to second-in-command of the Egyptian government.

The Bible is replete with stories of people who gave in to temptation and those who fled from it. Some, like David, experienced devastating results because of giving in. Others, like Joseph, did *not* succumb but still suffered—but imagine what his suffering would have been had he given in to the temptation.

> *We have the capacity for great sin. . . . We also have the capacity to do the right thing, even when it seems difficult at the time.*

These stories are important because we are both of these men. We have the capacity for great sin, which leads to a great fall and consequences that could haunt us for years in broken relationships, regret, or loss. We also have the capacity to do the right thing, even when it seems difficult at the time and brings unjust repercussions in the short run. And we have the gift to accept grace in all circumstances.

HOW TO FLEE: TEN WAYS TO RESIST TEMPTATION

Although we cannot avoid temptation, we can successfully resist it. The Bible promises, "Resist the devil [stand firm against him], and he will flee from you" (James 4:7 AMPC). You can be successful in overcoming temptation by focusing on the following ten principles.

1. *Know your enemy and his strategies.* In his sermon "Defeating Temptation," Gene Haraldsen shares a story from World War II about being familiar with one's enemy:

   Gen. George Patton of WWII fame was a great student of the history of warfare. During the battles of North Africa, Patton's troops and tanks were engaged in a series of attacks and counterattacks with the German Panzer Divisions under the command of Gen. Erwin Rommel, generally considered the greatest battlefield commander ever—up to that time.

Patton's forces did not fall for one of Rommel's traps, and in fact, successfully counterattacked and defeated the Germans. Patton watched the battle unfold, and at the moment he saw the battle turn, he stood up in his staff car and cried out, "I read your book. I read your book."

He was referring to Rommel's book on warfare called *Infantry Attacks*. Patton had learned of Rommel's strategy, had planned his moves accordingly, and defeated him.

Satan has written no books, but God has exposed the enemy's schemes in order that Satan might not outwit us.[9]

If you are not familiar with Satan's evil schemes against you, then you must learn his methods and the ways he tempts you (2 Cor. 2:11). Otherwise, he will gain the advantage over you, and you will lose the battle *and* the war.

2. *Watch out.* You must be alert at all times, like a soldier on watch. This means keeping your eyes focused on Jesus and being aware of potential threats to your fellowship with him. J. I. Packer explains the importance of this:

Christians must constantly be watchful and active against the Devil, for he is always at work trying to make them fall; whether by crushing them under the weight of hardship or pain or by urging them to a wrong fulfillment of natural desires, or by making them complacent, careless, and self-assertive, or by misrepresenting God to them and engendering false ideas of his truth and his will shows that Satan can even quote (and misapply) Scripture for this purpose.[10]

If you are not on guard against temptation, you will suffer a surprise attack.

3. *Rely on Jesus.* Remember that Jesus is on your side. Reflect on these words from Hebrews:

> Since then we have a great high priest who has passed through the heavens, Jesus, the Son of God, let us hold fast our confession. For we do not have a high priest who is unable to sympathize with our weaknesses, but one who in every respect has been tempted as we are, yet without sin. Let us then with confidence draw near to the throne of grace, that we may receive mercy and find grace to help in time of need. (Heb. 4:14–16)

Jesus faced temptation while he was on earth, and yet he did not sin. He understands your challenges, and he identifies with you. He is your High Priest, your advocate, before God. He is on your side!

4. *Pray.* Jesus says you should pray not to be led into temptation (Matt. 6:13). When you are tempted, ask for God's help. You need it! Jesus warned, "Be in prayer so you don't wander into temptation without even knowing you're in danger. There is a part of you that is eager, ready for anything in God. But there's another part that's as lazy as an old dog sleeping by the fire" (Matt. 26:41 MSG). In your prayers, confess your need for God and your desire to obey and honor him.

5. *Seek strength.* You need to know when you are weakest and most vulnerable to temptation. Sometimes it is when you have neglected your time with God or you are exhausted. In such moments, you may try to overcome temptation and avoid sin in your own power. This is futile and will result in failure.

The apostle Paul encourages you to seek Jesus and the power of the Holy Spirit when you face temptation: "I have strength for all things in Christ Who empowers me [I am ready for anything and equal to anything through Him Who infuses inner strength into me; I am self-sufficient in Christ's sufficiency]" (Phil. 4:13 AMPC). God will infuse you with the inner strength to resist temptation. Through him you can do anything!

This is why you must look to God's promises for strength. Meditate on them. Let them shift your thinking. For example, I often find inspiration in Isaiah 41:10: "Fear not, for I am with you; be not dismayed, for I am your God; I will strengthen you, I will help you, I will uphold you with my righteous right hand." When facing a tempting circumstance, I remember that God is with me and will help me in my hour of need. In this simple yet powerful reminder, I find the strength to say no.

6. *Be humble.* Although God made humanity very good (Gen. 1:31), we are all wired to sin because of the fall. Sin is now your natural tendency. If you become overconfident—a temptation for many leaders—and think you are above temptation, let God's Word correct you: "Therefore let anyone who thinks that he stands take heed lest he fall" (1 Cor. 10:12). Humbly admit that you can sin at any moment. As Exley notes, "Given the right circumstances, the best among us is capable of the most unimaginable sins."[11]

7. *Quote Scripture.* Memorize God's Word and use it to counter temptation. Jesus warded off the devil with Scripture when he was tempted in the wilderness (Matt. 4). There is no greater offensive weapon than Scripture to protect you from temptation. Take seriously the psalmist's words: "I have hidden your word in my heart, that I might not sin against you" (Ps. 119:11 NLT). If you know God's Word by heart, you will be able to recall Scriptures to deter temptation.

8. *Escape.* Look for a safe place to go when you face something enticing. Flee the situation. As Thomas à Kempis pointed out in *The Imitation of Christ,* "The only time to stop temptation is at the first point of recognition. If one begins to argue and engage in a hand-to-hand combat, temptation almost always wins the day."[12] Perhaps the usual "location" of your temptation is a circle of old friends, or it may be when you are alone stewing with your thoughts. Perhaps it is the high you get after a big achievement. Take action by fleeing. Do not linger on sin's doorstep.

9. *Trust God.* God is faithful and keeps his promises. He will not allow you to be tempted by more than you can bear (1 Cor. 10:13). He will also provide a way out. If he said it, he will do it. It is your job to trust him and take him at his word. Post God's promises

somewhere in your house or office where you will see them often, or set a daily reminder on your phone with a favorite promise from Scripture.

10. *Be accountable.* Leaders tend to keep their thoughts private. Temptations can build up in your imagination, and you might fantasize about the desired object. If you are not careful, your resolve will erode, and you will fall. You can prevent the erosion by allowing others to hold you accountable.

> *As a Christian leader, you must surround yourself with other believers who will regularly ask you tough questions about your life.*

The goal of accountability is to keep you on track in your walk with Jesus and reveal your inner struggles. As a Christian leader, you must surround yourself with other believers who will regularly ask you tough questions about your life. You need fellow believers with whom you can be transparent about your secret thought life.

Here are several questions I have found helpful in staying accountable with my Christian brothers and maintaining my integrity:

» *Successes and failures.* Did you experience any wins or make mistakes this week? What's working or not working? What will you amplify, improve, or change?
» *Quiet times.* How often did you read your Bible, meditate, and pray this week? What did you learn? What will you do differently?
» *Confession.* Are you regularly confessing your sins to God? Are you specific and repentant? If yes, what has been the benefit? If not, why?
» *Fellowship.* Are you growing closer or further apart in your relationship with Jesus? Why? How about with your Christian brothers and sisters?

» *Integrity.* Are you who you say you are at home? At work? If so, how? If not, why? Do you do what you say you will do? Why or why not?

» *Private thought life.* What is consuming your thoughts? What are you anxious about?

» *Temptation.* What are you wrestling with, and how are you addressing it?

» *Generosity.* How have you given of your time, talents, and resources to advance God's kingdom and help others?

» *Relationships.* How are your personal and professional relationships? Which ones are going well, and which need improving?

» *Witness.* Have you had a chance to share your faith with someone? If so, tell me about it. If not, are you praying for an opportunity?

» *Reality check.* Have you been honest and forthright about your answers? If not, what's preventing you?

» *Reciprocity.* How can I pray for you?

Since temptation is a frequent challenge for discipled leaders—as for all Christians—it is critical that we know how to handle temptations successfully. I hope that these ten suggestions will help you the next time you are tempted to do something you know you shouldn't.

Always remember: You do not have to give in to temptation and sin. As a Christian, you have the power of the Holy Spirit who lives in you. You can overcome temptation through reliance on Jesus. God promises that you do not have to fall flat on your face. He will provide a way out of temptation so you can escape and resist it.

Discipled leaders know that temptation leads to sin and sin has consequences. The law of consequences says that you reap what you sow, meaning that every action produces an outcome, good or bad. The Bible asks the rhetorical question, "Can a man scoop a flame into his lap and not have his clothes catch on fire?" (Prov. 6:27 NLT). Of course not!

To this day, I am so glad I did not "scoop a flame" into my lap by telling Don exactly what I thought about his feedback. I have to imagine that my professional life would certainly have caught fire had I fallen into that temptation. By God's grace, I was instead able to flee the temptation before me.

HOW I FLED

After the twelfth time I slammed the phone down without having called Don back, I took a deep breath. I chose to write a different conclusion to the story that had been playing out in my head—the one where I stormed into Don's office and proved to him just how wrong he was about me and my communication skills.

Instead, I paused, breathed, and *prayed*. We have already talked about the importance of prayer, but this was not so much about the fact that I prayed, but what I prayed for. I asked God for help to overcome my emotions and exercise self-control. And I began reflecting. *Maybe Don was right. Maybe the presentation was flat, and I didn't connect with the audience. I was too emotional. Pride got in my way, and I became defensive.* I realized that Don had been trying to help me improve. Lastly, I thought about the inevitable high cost had I called Don and told him what I thought.

I did not call him. Nor did I ever mention his call to him. Instead, I internalized his feedback and worked on improving how I presented on the phone. I no longer overprepared or wrote scripts. I developed talking points and delivered each presentation conversationally.

Don began receiving a lot of positive feedback about my delivery. Some people even said I was inspiring. In time, Don asked me to help him present at other meetings.

Thank you, Lord, for keeping me off that phone, for shutting my mouth, and for helping me flee from the temptation to prove my superiority.

Temptations in the workplace come in all shapes and sizes. In my experience with Don, I learned some invaluable lessons about exercising self-control and effectively responding to criticism. At some point, all leaders receive slaps on the wrist—disapproval for a mistake or a shortcoming. And specifically because leaders have positions of influence, we often feel a temptation to pride, to ignore feedback, or to respond aggressively when we know others are looking to us to be confident and strong. When you face criticism and the desire to retaliate, or you encounter any other workplace temptation, consider applying the following principles.

- *Manage your emotions.* Leaders should expect to be criticized. Reflecting on Abraham Lincoln's presidency, Michael McKinney says, "Any leader will be criticized. How you handle it will determine whether you succeed or fail."[13] When you receive feedback, remain humble, keep a sense of humor, and do not get defensive. Stay confident and composed and do not take the criticism personally. Consider the ramifications of striking back. Have the presence of mind to determine whether or not you should respond. Ask yourself, In the grand scheme of things, will my response make a difference? Take to heart the Bible words that "Whoever is slow to anger is better than the mighty, and he who rules his spirit than he who takes a city" (Prov. 16:32).

  Other temptations also arise in the workplace during times of high emotion, such as missing a deadline, having to reprimand a team member, or watching a project fall apart. It is often under stress that we want to shift blame, cut corners, go behind someone's back, or burn bridges. As a leader in charge of a team environment, you must recognize and name your own emotions. Whether you are angry, tired, discouraged, resentful, or cocky, remember that your feelings will change. You do not have to act on your emotions in the moment. Figure out what works best for you to keep your emotions under control. Maybe you need to step back and get alone with God, go for a run, or call a trusted friend.
- *Listen for the truth.* Not all criticism is valid, but most criticism contains a grain of truth. Consider the source. If the person criticizing you is credible and wants what is best for you, listen intently. If not, look for the truth grains. Take what is real and meaningful. Reject what is not. Ask someone you trust if you warranted the criticism, and seek the thoughts of that person. This is the course of wisdom: "Without counsel plans fail, but with many advisers, they succeed" (Prov. 15:22).

  Remember that the most convincing lies—and temptations—

have an element of truth to them. That is why too often we believe them. Discernment is essential; when you feel tempted in the workplace, pause and pray for God's insight into the real heart of the issue.

- *Make a change.* If the criticism is justified, determine how you can improve. Reflect on how the feedback can help you. Commit to making a positive change that will benefit you and others. Let your improvement silence the critics. Lastly, accept that no matter what you do, some people may not be pleased.

All leaders face deserved criticism, and all leaders fall into temptation. Failure can feel paralyzing, especially when we have been tempted repeatedly and failed in the same area. But do not let that failure define you. God can use all things together for those who love him. Whatever temptations you face in the workplace, take your failure to God, let him pick you up and dust you off again, determine to learn from your mistakes, and set a practical goal for overcoming the temptation next time. God's Spirit is sanctifying you and working to conform you into the image of his Son, Jesus.

If you manage your emotions, listen to the truth, and make a change, you will be able to handle criticism well, face your temptations, and be a composed leader.

COUNTING THE COST

In the hours, days, and weeks that followed that conference call and Don's feedback on my presentation, God kept impressing a question on my mind: "Is it worth it?" I took that to mean two things: Is obedience worth the reward? And is sin worth the risk?

Discipled leaders are aware of the physical and emotional states that make them vulnerable to temptation—like hunger, anger, loneliness, and tiredness. If your guard is down, you may be more likely to be enticed. Also, discipled leaders decide to remain obedient to God and not sin *before* the temptation arises. They think ahead and ask themselves, Is it worth it?

- Is it worth losing your spouse and everything you have over an affair?
- Is it worth losing your job because of falsifying records?
- Is it worth destroying a relationship by getting revenge or holding a grudge?
- Is it worth losing intimacy with your spouse by watching pornography in your hotel room?
- Is it worth getting drunk or high to escape life?

Of course not! But the flesh, the devil, and the world deceive us into thinking we are not making as bad of a decision as we really are. Yet we all know of well-known figures who have suffered a great fall because of one bad choice. As Richard Exley writes, "Few things in life are more painful than a moral failure. . . . Kings have renounced their thrones, saints their God, and spouses their lifetime partners. People have been known to sell their souls, jobs, reputations, children, marriage—they have chucked everything for a brief moment of pleasure."[14]

As a leader, you know that it only takes a moment to do great harm. Take seriously this fact. But take heart! If you are tempted, the great news is that God is faithful and will not allow you to be tempted beyond what you can stand. He will also provide a way out so you can endure it (1 Cor. 10:13). But if you do sin, know that God is full of grace. That is why discipled leaders confess sin to the Lord.

Know that you can live a victorious life through the power of the Holy Spirit, and the rewards are great. "Blessed (happy, to be envied) is the man who is patient under trial and stands up under temptation, for when he has stood the test and been approved, he will receive [the victor's] crown of life which God has promised to those who love Him" (James 1:12 AMPC).

When you face temptation, ask yourself, "Is it worth it?"

Then think—and pray—before you act.

QUESTIONS

- How would you describe your experiences of testing and temptation since becoming a Christian? What are the most difficult tests or temptations you face?

- Have you ever thought about the consequences of sin? What are your "Is it worth it?" questions?
- What specific steps do you need to take to improve your success in handling testing and temptation? When will you take these steps?
- How do you practice accountability in your life? Whom could you ask to partner with, if you don't currently have a regular accountability practice?
- How well do you handle criticism? How can you improve?
- When did you last lose your composure? What happened? What role does self-control play in leadership and why is it important?
- How will these discipleship and leadership principles help you transform your workplace through your pursuit of Christ?

CHAPTER SEVEN

STAND

As a disciple, stand tall.

As a leader, overcome fear with faith.

*Finally, be strong in the Lord and in his mighty power. Put on
the full armor of God, so that you can take your stand against the
devil's schemes. For our struggle is not against flesh and blood, but
against the rulers, against the authorities, against the powers of this
dark world and against the spiritual forces of evil in the heavenly
realms. Therefore put on the full armor of God, so that when the
day of evil comes, you may be able to stand your ground, and
after you have done everything, to stand.*

—EPHESIANS 6:10–13 NIV

SOMETIMES *PLACING AN* obstacle in the road is the right choice. As a leader, I feel strange writing that, but it is the truth—literally.

My friend Mike and I stood at the school bus stop near my home in Knoxville, Tennessee, surveying the curved hill before us. I spoke what we both were thinking: "I can't believe how fast the cars zoom down the hill toward the bus stop. Between the speeding cars, the blind curve, and the bus stop location, we've got an accident waiting to happen. We ought to put in a speed sign and speed hump to slow folks down."

Mike laughed. "Never gonna happen! Do you know *anything* about the developer, Mr. Ruffian?"

I shook my head.

"He wants control." Mike elongated the last word so I would understand just how much control Mr. Ruffian wanted. "Me and some of the other neighbors have complained about that part of the road multiple times to him, but he's refused to do anything. I've resorted to yelling at people to slow down. One day, I threw water balloons at the cars to get the drivers' attention." Mike gave me a smug look.

I just thought, *Doesn't that compound the situation?*

"He has a tombstone mentality, Preston. He won't make any changes like adding a speed hump unless there's an accident or someone dies. If the idea isn't his, he won't do anything. And if he's challenged or confronted, he'll fight to get his way—even if he's wrong. It's not worth your time."

I may not have known Mr. Ruffian, but it seemed that Mike did not really know me either. *Possibly saving kids' lives isn't worth my time battling an egomaniac?*

Mike, Mr. Ruffian, and the neighborhood were all about to get to know me.

I looked Mike square in the eye. "I think we can make a change. Wait and see. We'll have a speed hump here in one year."

"Yeah right, Preston. Good luck."

Within the week, I had contacted the county's traffic engineering department, learning that I would need a signed petition, a traffic study, a preliminary plan design, a public meeting, resident voting, and then finally implementation.

That's a lot of work for a speed hump.

I enlisted a group of neighbors to secure enough signatures on our petition. Then the county conducted a traffic study at the future-fatal-accident site and found that 85 percent of the drivers on that stretch were exceeding the speed limit! The county then confirmed that the hill and blind curve were a safety hazard. Their suggested plan was to install eight speed humps throughout the neighborhood. (I thought eight was overkill, but I figured they knew what they were doing.)

I was surprised that we had not encountered any roadblocks yet. But we also had not gotten to the most important part of the process: the public meeting. The county's plan required 70 percent of my neighbors to vote yes to their proposal. That meant 350 out of 500 homes would have to cast an affirmative vote.

Certainly, 350 families would want to keep their loved ones safe, right?

Well, there was at least one family—or at least one man—who had other motivating factors.

The county set the public meeting for early December. Upon arriving home after our Thanksgiving vacation, I found this flyer in my mail:

CONGRATULATIONS NEIGHBORHOOD PROPERTY
OWNERS: SPEED CAMERAS ARE COMING!
In the event you have not heard, our neighborhood has been hijacked by a small group of "dedicated property owners" who

have described our community as "totally unsafe." These "dedicated property owners" have asked for speed bumps and speed cameras to be installed!

A plethora of speed bumps, coupled with speed cameras, means that our neighborhood residents will create a nice addition to the county's revenue for the next fiscal year. A worthy endeavor!

Vote "NO" to Preston Poore's personal quest to install speed bumps and cameras throughout our neighborhood (rest assured, there will not be one in front of his home!).

Who will pay for this—are you willing to see a property tax increase and pay speeding tickets? Vote "NO" on the "traffic calming" nonsense! There is a meeting on December 5th at the clubhouse.

BIG BROTHER MUST BE STOPPED!

I could not believe it. In addition to the personal attack, the flyer was full of lies. The county's plan did not include speed cameras, speed monitoring, or speed bumps—which are technically different from speed humps.

Thank God for the team I had assembled. I called a few members to discuss the flyer, and a few members had called me since the flyer had gone to everyone in the neighborhood. In the midst of my fear and doubt about continuing on, they encouraged me to keep fighting. They all knew we needed this change in our neighborhood. They even went so far as to call all the "traffic-calming-plan backers" in our area to remind them about the importance of the upcoming meeting.

I was not going to give up. I was not going to stop. I was not going to let a bully like Mr. Ruffian allow a selfish decision to override doing the right thing.

THE WAR YOU CANNOT ESCAPE

Before I tell you how my epic battle with Mr. Ruffian turned out, we need to consider a battle that truly is epic: the war for your soul.

Whether or not you realize it, you have always been in a spiritual war. Before you became a Christian, your eyes were closed to the battle because your heart, mind, and soul were blindly conformed to the world. You were no threat to the opposition. But when you became a Christian and surrendered your life to Christ, God opened your eyes to another realm. And the opposition took notice.

> *Your fight is not against flesh and blood*
> *but against the unseen powers of darkness. This war*
> *is a real and serious daily struggle.*

Now you are a targeted soldier engaged in the struggle between God and the rebellion of Satan, good overcoming evil, light triumphing over darkness. Your fight is not against flesh and blood but against the unseen powers of darkness. This war is a real and serious daily struggle. The Bible calls it "no weekend war that we'll walk away from and forget about in a couple of hours. This is for keeps, a life-or-death fight to the finish against the Devil and all his angels" (Eph. 6:12 MSG). This war does not come and go—it is a lifetime battle. Genuine Christianity requires full commitment and a determination to stand. There is no neutral ground.

As you engage in this war, you need to know who your enemy is, you need to understand and use the equipment and tools you have been given, and you need to know where you get your strength.

KNOW YOUR ENEMY

A long time ago, an angel named Lucifer was in heaven. This "light bearer" was called "Day Star, son of Dawn" (Isa. 14:12).[1] Lucifer occupied an exalted position in the heavens, but something happened in heaven that changed everything. Lucifer became proud. He desired to occupy God's throne. (If this sounds familiar, pride is the same sin Satan tempted Adam and Eve with in the garden of Eden!) We do not know why or how pride overcame this exalted angel of light. As Martyn

Lloyd-Jones notes, the Bible "does not explain how these thoughts ever entered into the heart of Satan, the devil. It simply tells us that they did. The Bible gives us no explanation as to the ultimate origin of evil."[2]

Because of Lucifer's rebellion, he was cast out of heaven, along with the other angels who supported him. He eventually became known as Satan, which means "adversary," the enemy of God. He is also called the devil, which means "accuser," because he charges God's people with fault or blame.

Satan is a powerful, cunning, and creative enemy. He will use anything and everything at his disposal to oppose God. He hates God and hates you because of Christ in you. You must never underestimate his ability. Satan and his army are always ready to attack. His agenda is to undermine God's will, authority, and kingdom expansion, and he accomplishes it in several ways.

- *Devouring you.* The Bible calls Satan an adversary, who "prowls around like a roaring lion, seeking someone to devour" (1 Peter 5:8). J. I. Packer writes, "Satan and his devils exhibit unimaginable meanness, malice, fury, and cruelty directed against God, against God's truth, and against those to whom God has extended his saving love."[3] Satan's efforts are all aimed at destroying your faith in God. He may plant seeds of doubt in your mind, build up your pride so you think you do not need God, or sidetrack you with worldly pursuits like riches, celebrity, or power.
- *Dampening your love for God.* The great theologian John Wesley describes the devil's work as striving "to stifle our love of God, as he knows this is the spring of all our religion, and that, as this rises or falls, the work of God flourishes or decays in the soul."[4] Satan wants nothing more than for your love for God to grow cold.
- *Stealing your life.* Satan is a thief, who "comes only to steal and kill and destroy" (John 10:10). Satan wants to take life from you—your purpose, your meaning, your well-being, your joy, your strength. He wants you to feel insignificant, useless, empty, despairing, and dissatisfied.
- *Diminishing your love for your neighbor.* Wesley describes how Satan

takes aim at our love for others: "Satan desires to excite either private or public suspicions, animosities, resentment, quarrels; to destroy the peace of families or of nations; and to banish unity and concord from the earth."[5] Jesus taught that we should treat all people as neighbors, with compassion and mercy (Luke 10:25–37), but Satan will do anything to stop you from sharing God's love and kindness with those around you.

- *Hindering God's work in you.* Satan wants to keep you from growing in grace and in the knowledge of our Lord Jesus Christ (2 Peter 3:18). Think about your quiet times with God. They are an extremely valuable opportunity to connect with God through reading the Bible and praying. God works in you as you commune with him. He reveals who he is and develops Christlike character in you. But Satan has a different agenda: he wants to stunt your growth. Have you ever thought, on any given day, that you would rather not read your Bible and pray? Maybe once you decide to pass on spending time with God and turn the TV on instead. The next day you find another excuse not to connect with God. Over time, your quiet times become sporadic and eventually stop. You have cut off one of your most valuable ways to connect with God. Satan may well have been behind the scenes, manipulating circumstances to divert your time and attention from connecting with God on a daily basis. Eventually, you lost motivation and Satan accomplished his goal of hindering God's work in you.

- *Tempting you to sin.* Satan is a liar. He seduces you by making sin look good in your eyes, which leads to evil behaviors and away from God.

- *Making you ineffective.* Satan and his demons will find your weaknesses, accuse you when you sin, and make you feel guilty. To make you ineffective, he will lead you to despair, disappointment, and discouragement and away from repentance. He wants shame and fear to get in the way of your relationship with God and with close family and friends.

- *Disengaging you from the Great Commission.* Satan does not want you to spread the gospel of Christ. He wants you to view witnessing as an inconvenience or something that other Christians will take care of.

- *Destroying the church.* Satan will plant false doctrine, create division among God's people through scandals, spread rumors to stir dissension, persecute its members, or even kill them to prevent God's work.

This bully is relentless and only wants to harm you. Fortunately, God has given us specific spiritual protection. He has provided spiritual armor to protect us where we are vulnerable: the heart, mind, and soul.

PREPARING FOR THE FIGHT

God provides protection for the spiritual battles you will face as you fight on the front lines. Using the example of a Roman soldier, the apostle Paul describes the six pieces of equipment you must put on and wear daily.

- *The belt of truth.* This represents the reality of who God is. When the enemy attacks us with lies, deception, and half-truths, we must rely on the truth of what God has done, who he is, and what he has promised to do. The belt of truth holds all of the other armor together, integrating God's power in your life. As you trust God and walk in integrity, you do not need to fear your enemies.[6]
- *The breastplate of righteousness.* A breastplate is the piece of physical body armor that covered soldiers from the neck to the waist, both front and back. In spiritual armor, it represents your right relationship with God and your right living in Christ. Jesus became sin for us so that we "might become the righteousness of God" (2 Cor. 5:21). Because of Christ's sacrifice, you are righteous in God's sight. However, you can still become vulnerable to your enemy's attacks when you sin, lose sight of God's truth, and walk away from him. If you are right with God, you will be able to fight and stand. If you are full of sin, you will be weighted down and unable to fight.[7]
- *The "gospel of peace" shoes.* These refer to the shin guards or shoes

worn by soldiers to protect their legs and feet. "Gospel of peace" shoes help Christians walk through rough paths on the way to sharing the gospel. Though times may get tough, the Christian should always be prepared to share the gospel.[8] As Wiersbe puts it, "The most victorious Christian is a witnessing Christian."[9]

- *The shield of faith.* The shield Paul refers to was not a small, handheld piece with limited protection. It was a rather large shield, four feet by two feet, constructed of wood and covered with leather. A soldier would hold it and ward off spears, arrows, or fiery darts. Your faith in Jesus acts as a shield that protects you from doubt and temptations.[10]

- *The helmet of salvation.* The helmet protected the head and neck. The "helmet of salvation" refers to the assurance of your salvation and your victory in Christ. You have a hope and confidence that will not be shaken. The helmet also protects your mind from Satan's attempts to have you question God's power, love, or commitment to you.

- *The sword of the Spirit.* This is the only offensive weapon God gives us, and Paul says it is the word of God (Eph. 6:17). Warren Wiersbe describes its effectiveness:

> A material sword pierces the body, but the Word of God pierces the heart. The more you use a physical sword, the duller it becomes; but using God's Word only makes it sharper in our lives. . . . A physical sword wounds to hurt and kill, while the sword of the Spirit wounds to heal and give life. But when we use the sword against Satan, we are out to deal him a blow that will cripple him and keep him from hindering God's work.[11]

To effectively use your sword, you must know God's Word through reading, study, and memorization. The more you do, the stronger you will be.

When you are protected by the armor of God, you are ready to stand against what Satan and the world are sure to hurl at you. To stand in this way means to act as conquerors—keeping the field, not being beaten down, nor giving way.[12] It means being a force for good. In God's power, you can help restore the world and its citizens to the way God intended: right, orderly, just, abundant, beautiful, flourishing, full of life. You can help create a culture where people care less about self and more about others. Where love replaces hate. Where peace triumphs over war. Where people can come to know Jesus, grow to be like him, and serve him without barriers. Where chains are broken and lives are healed. Stand tall for your faith.

TEN TACTICS OF SPIRITUAL WARFARE

Clad in the armor of God, you need not fear Satan. You are assured of Christ's victory in the long run—but the battles will not be easy. The next time you face spiritual bullying by the devil, consider applying one (or all) of these ten tactics of spiritual warfare. Through these strategies, you can overcome the daily schemes of your enemy.

1. *Submit to God.* "Submit yourselves therefore to God" (James 4:7). This is where you start. You must humble yourself before God, confess your sins, and seek him. Your spirit is safest and most sheltered when you live by the wisdom that God's ways are best, and you trust his love and guidance.
2. *Rely on God's power.* "Be strong in the Lord and in the strength of his might" (Eph. 6:10). As a believer, you are filled with the Holy Spirit. So trust God. He will fill you with power and strength. Your strength does not come from yourself—your education, money, influence, or fame. Trusting in yourself will lead to defeat. If you trust in God, he will give you what you need to win. If he is for you, who can be against you? There is no match for his power.
3. *Stay connected.* You are on the front line in a war and need to stay in constant contact with your commander, God. The apostle Paul encourages us to be "praying at all times in the Spirit, with all prayer and supplication" (Eph. 6:18). Make prayer part of your daily life and stay connected to God.

4. *Resist the devil.* James told believers to "resist the devil, and he will flee from you" (James 4:7). How do you resist? By running to God. Draw close to him, and he will draw close to you (v. 8). Refuse Satan and in the Holy Spirit's power say, "No!" After you have run to God, he will lift you up. With God's help, you can withstand or counteract Satan's attacks and he will leave.

5. *Guard your heart.* You must protect your heart—your mind, will, and emotions—above all else, "for it determines the course of your life" (Prov. 4:23 NLT). Do not let sin seep in and desensitize you to God. Thoughts control actions. If you think sinful, bad, negative, or unhealthy thoughts, you will produce sinful, bad, negative, and unhealthy actions. Guarding your heart means intentionally dwelling on Christlike thoughts to produce Christlike actions in your life.

6. *Stay alert.* The apostle Peter writes, "Stay alert! Watch out for your great enemy, the devil" (1 Peter 5:8 NLT). Satan is always on the prowl. He has two plans of attack: when you are ready and when you are not! Do not let pride make you think you are immune to temptation or will not sin in a certain area. Remain vigilant and do not succumb to his attacks.

7. *Expect trials.* You should expect "fiery trials" and suffering in your life—after all, you are engaged in a battle (1 Peter 4:12 NLT). Do not be surprised by them. The key is to look to God for his protection and peace in the midst of them. God is sovereign and faithful, even when we may not feel like he is in control.

8. *Deny a foothold.* Paul warned Christians not to "give the devil a foothold" (Eph. 4:27 NIV). Do not give Satan any place in your life where he can get a grip, where he can find a place or an opportunity to attack you. You must drop your resentment, forgive others and seek forgiveness, control your anger, and replace worry with worship. Deal with your negative emotions immediately. If you do not, Satan will turn a foothold into a stronghold.

9. *Be courageous.* You do not need to be afraid because God is with you. Take comfort in his words: "Have I not commanded you? Be strong and courageous. Do not be frightened, and do not be dismayed,

for the LORD your God is with you wherever you go" (Josh. 1:9). Courage is acting in the presence of fear. You must have the courage to fight.

10. *Remember God's promises.* God promises that you will be victorious and that *nothing* will separate you from him. The apostle Paul writes of this truth in one of Scripture's most comforting promises:

Who shall separate us from the love of Christ? Shall tribulation, or distress, or persecution, or famine, or nakedness, or danger, or sword? As it is written, "For your sake we are being killed all the day long; we are regarded as sheep to be slaughtered." No, in all these things we are more than conquerors through him who loved us. For I am sure that neither death nor life, nor angels nor rulers, nor things present nor things to come, nor powers, nor height nor depth, nor anything else in all creation, will be able to separate us from the love of God in Christ Jesus our Lord. (Rom. 8:35–39)

You are fighting as a **result** *of victory,*
not to **achieve** *victory.*

While you fight, always remember this empowering truth: you are fighting as a *result* of victory, not to *achieve* victory. Satan is a conquered foe, defeated by Christ's death and resurrection, and he will ultimately be destroyed. Jesus's sacrifice defeated Satan, his army, and sin. He "disarmed the spiritual rulers and authorities. He shamed them publicly by his victory over them on the cross" (Col. 2:15 NLT). The war has already been won. It is from this victory and through God's power that you fight.

Jesus is infinitely more powerful than Satan. The one "who is in you is greater than he who is in the world" (1 John 4:4). Satan has limitations because he is a created being and not God. He is not God's equal. Satan is not all-powerful like God. Satan is not all-knowing like God. Satan is not all-present like God. He is powerful and smart, and he has great influence in the world, but he is not God.

In other words, God will win. No doubt.

OVERCOMING FEAR

God will win the war, but we still have to fight the daily battle. As a leader, you may even face more personal and professional battles than those you lead, and many of these battles involve fear. You might feel the temptation to redefine right and wrong so you will not "fall behind" your sales goals. You might become discouraged because of professional setbacks and begin to doubt your abilities to grow and adapt. You might worry about being seen as weak, so you hide your weaknesses and mistakes. Tensions with team members may make you feel like they won't hear you anyway, so why make the effort to communicate or offer feedback?

Discipled leaders overcome fear through faith. They understand that fear or faith will rule their hearts and minds depending on which one they feed the most.

Fear is a powerful human emotion that impacts everyone, including leaders, and it comes in many different forms—including failure, success, dying, commitment, public speaking, rejection, making the wrong decision, criticism, taking responsibility, and the unknown. Other fears include being found out or exposed, not fitting in, being stuck in a current role, being disliked, being fired, not living up to expectations, making people mad, conflict, being honest, and fearing what others think. This is a pretty exhaustive list.

Anticipation of physical harm or a perceived threat triggers fear. Fear elicits physical responses like sweating, rapid heartbeat, and weakness. Apprehension creates doubts, insecurity, and low self-esteem. Fright also evokes apathy, inaction, and ignorance. Chronic fear can impact your overall well-being. Fear can cripple and render you ineffective.

I learned a long time ago that *fear* stands for "false evidence appearing real," meaning that one's perceptions drive negative emotions and thinking. For example, everyone engages in a daily conversation with themselves. Studies show that we have "12,000 to 60,000 thoughts per day. . . . As many as 98 percent of them are exactly the same as we had the day before."[13] This self-talk is often unconstructive and damaging—eight out of ten thoughts we have each day are negative.[14] Do the math. That's up to 48,000 negative thoughts daily. Don't believe me? Think about the lies your inner critic tells you every day:

- I am unworthy.
- I can't lead.
- I am a failure.
- I'm not good enough.
- No one loves me or cares for me.
- I don't belong anywhere.
- I have no purpose.
- I'm weak.
- This will never work.
- I must be perfect.
- It's too late to pursue my dream.

The battle against fear begins in your mind. With all the negative thoughts, where do you turn? How do you overcome fear? Discipled leaders overcome fear through faith. They understand that fear or faith will rule their hearts and minds depending on which one they feed the most. If they feed their fear, it will dominate. If they feed their faith, fear will diminish. Activate your faith; seek God in times of despair, doubt, panic, or terror; and take that step forward in confidence. Take specific action to accomplish this.

- *Stop negative self-talk.* Avoid listening to your inner critic and begin listening to your "inner champion" by intentionally shifting toward more Christ-centered and positive thoughts every day. What if your self-talk sounded more like this:

- » Because of Christ, I am worthy.
- » I can lead.
- » I am successful.
- » I'm good enough.
- » I'm loved and cared for.
- » I do belong.
- » I have purpose.
- » I'm strong.
- » This will work.
- » I can make mistakes.
- » It's never too late to pursue my dream.

If you reframe your thoughts, silence your inner critic, and listen to the inner champion, you will be on the path to overcoming fear and developing confidence. You will be more apt to share your ideas in meetings, collaborate with others, build trust, empower your team, communicate effectively, and make sound decisions.

- *Define your fear.* Identify what is holding you back. What frightens you? The more you know about something, the more confident you become. Use this simple formula to determine what is preventing you from moving forward:

  - » *What frightens me the most is . . .* (e.g., losing my job).
  - » *It frightens me because . . .* (e.g., If I do, I won't be able to pay my bills).
  - » *Because I haven't dealt with my fear, I feel . . .* (e.g., anxious, hopeless, sleepless, depressed).
  - » *If I face my fear and take action to overcome it . . .* (e.g., my well-being will improve, and I will experience peace).

- *Remember the future.* Think back to your previous accomplishments or challenges, and remember how God was faithful. Recall times you were fearful and how you relied on God's promises. You only need to look backward to see forward. Imagine yourself a couple of years from now successfully overcoming your fear and achieving your objective. Write a headline about what will be said about how you rose above the fear. What will you have accomplished? What victory will you have experienced? How did you succeed?

- *Take constructive steps.* Develop a plan to gain exposure to the thing you fear the most. For example, if you are afraid of public speaking, enroll in a public speaking course. Then begin looking for small opportunities to present to others. You will gain experience that may lead to bigger opportunities, and you will gain confidence as you build your capabilities.

An additional challenge for leaders is that fear is infectious, and followers will not support or commit to you if they sense your fear. On the other hand, courage is just as contagious, and people will follow if they see your courage, if you step out despite the uncertainties.

THE REST OF THE STORY

I experienced both infectious fear and contagious courage in my battle against Mr. Ruffian. When I received the accusatory flyer, I was shocked and angry. But as the day of the neighborhood meeting approached, I grew afraid. At the meeting, where more than a hundred people had packed the neighborhood clubhouse, my fear of losing increased exponentially.

I recognized many of the neighbors, along with Mr. Ruffian. Supporters and opposition were both in attendance. But there were also some strangers in the room, which seemed odd. I opened the meeting and introduced the county representative. Suddenly, some of the strangers began booing. They were heckling me and stirring up the crowd! I looked over to Mr. Ruffian. He smirked diabolically. The strangers were his henchmen.

After a series of back-and-forth remarks between supporters and the opposition, I regained control of the meeting. I asked the attendees to remain silent and allow the county representative to present the traffic-calming plan. Then I asked the crowd to be patient because we would conduct a question-and-answer session after the presentation.

When I opened up the room for discussion, Mr. Ruffian's henchmen agitated the supporters with ridiculous questions and accusations. After an intense thirty minutes, I thanked everyone for their interest and reminded the attendees about the vote. We needed 350 or 70 percent of the residents to vote yes for it to pass. I wished them a good night and left.

I was emotionally and physically worn out after the meeting. I felt like I had been maltreated for trying to do the right thing. I also doubted that the plan would pass. In the midst of my self-pity and doubt, I prayed and asked God for his help. I knew the vote was in his hands, and all I could do was wait for the result.

Two weeks later, the county called. The traffic-calming plan had only received 300 yeses or 60 percent of the required votes, well short of our goal. I had failed. I felt like I had let down the supporters. Discouraged, I wanted to quit. But the bus stop was still a dangerous area. Something needed to be done, but how? We had gone through the county's exhausting approval process to no avail.

Then I started thinking, *We can't give up. There must be a solution. This bully can't win.* A majority of the neighbors *had* voted for the plan, even though it was by a narrow margin. I thought I could challenge the county about the high vote percentage threshold they had established. Also, I thought I should remind the county that the traffic study had revealed a safety concern, yet the issue remained unresolved. With such a concern, the county was obligated to act.

Still, the situation appeared hopeless. I prayed again and asked God to intervene. I also reminded myself that losing the fight did not mean the war was over and that being afraid of failure was not a good enough reason for not facing my fears and keeping the neighborhood safe. I ran my thoughts by some of the plan's supporters. They agreed and believed I should approach the county one more time. I set up a meeting with the head of the county traffic engineering department and stated my case. After generously listening to my points, he said, "I agree with you, and we'll move forward with placing one speed hump on the hill. The installation will take place in two months."

Flabbergasted, I asked him, "Can you install the speed hump without neighborhood approval?"

"Yes. We confirmed a safety concern, the county is required to solve the problem, and it's the right thing to do. We've got it from here. Thanks for your help!"

Can I tell you how gratifying it was to hear that, and particularly to hear him use the phrase, "It's the right thing to do"?

In one way, the battle for the speed hump had already been won as soon as the county completed the traffic study that confirmed the safety hazard. But I still had to fight through the accusations, intimidation, and disappointment of the misleading flyers and the trumped-up neighborhood meeting. If I had believed the lies, given in to fear, or let discouragement have the final word, then I would not have approached the head of county traffic, and the speed hump would've never become a reality. I had to keep fighting, remembering that the truth was truth, whether or not I felt it in the moment, and relying on God's strength to keep me going.

Finally, after additional resistance from Mr. Ruffian—including a lawsuit threat—the county installed the speed hump. God was faithful! In the midst of the challenges and doubt, he was with me all of the way. Through him, I found the courage to act in the presence of fear and complete the play.

After the speed-hump installation, I stood with Mike at the bus stop. It had been about a year since he had first questioned my resolve. We watched cars slow down as they drove past.

I looked at Mike. "Not worth my time, eh?"

Mike laughed. "Every bully gets his due."

Every time I see or ride over that speed hump, I smile and remember it as a spiritual marker. God helped me stand tall. He gave me the courage to overcome fear with faith. And he helped me see that I can fight the daily battles of the discipled life with the same confidence.

QUESTIONS

- Are you experiencing spiritual warfare? If so, how do you know? Are you winning or losing? If you are losing, what can you do?
- What are your greatest fears? How do they impact you? How can you begin to overcome them?

- What role does courage play in leadership, and why is it important?
- Have you experienced bullying or intimidation? What is your story? How might the discipled leadership principles presented here help?
- How will these discipleship and leadership principles help you transform your workplace through your pursuit of Christ?

CHAPTER EIGHT

CHOOSE

As a disciple, choose joy.

As a leader, delight others.

I have told you these things, that My joy and delight may be in you, and that your joy and gladness may be of full measure and complete and overflowing.

—JOHN 15:11 AMPC

On a fateful Monday morning, the subject line of the first email that popped into my inbox read, "Defective Displays—Need Solution." I clicked and saw a picture of one of our promotional display units collapsed. *One defect doesn't mean something's defective*, I thought. *One collapsing display out of eight thousand doesn't mean there's a problem.*

I had just arrived back in my office after a long vacation. I was tan, rested, and ready to go, especially considering that our most significant promotion of the year was in progress. My team was accountable for designing, producing, and delivering more than eight thousand display units to support the promotion. Each unit had an innovative triangular design, and its durability had been thoroughly tested in our quality-assurance process. It was a million-dollar company investment. Meeting our financial goals—and maybe even my professional future—hinged on the success of this promotion.

Dozens more emails arrived. Phones rang in the background. Every ding and buzz told me what I did not want to admit: It was not just one collapsing display. They were failing all across the country.

Since the display unit was supporting our multimillion-dollar promotion, my team had to act quickly. I contacted Craig, the project manager. Before anything else, we needed to determine the problem's scale, cause, and potential solutions. To our surprise, we learned that consumers were aggressively digging into the displays, looking for our product emblazoned with their name. Additionally, the displays bulged if overfilled. They were not designed for either stressor. So much for quality assurance!

Craig walked into my office, his face pale. "This mistake is going to cost over a million dollars. I'm going to lose my job over this!" He could not see a path forward—only one leading to crisis and failure.

THE SUFFICIENCY OF GRACE

When we rely on something—even a promotional display—and it gives way, we can feel burned, discouraged, and uncertain. Sometimes we even stop believing things will improve in the future. We stop seeing what blessings we do have.

In high school, I discovered that I had inherited a genetic disease called Charcot-Marie-Tooth disease (CMT), a neuromuscular disease that affects the peripheral nerves outside the brain and spinal cord. The disease causes muscle weakness and atrophy and some loss of sensation in the feet, lower legs, hands, and forearms. CMT symptoms may include foot deformity (very high arched feet), foot drop (the inability to hold the foot horizontal), a "slapping" gait (the slap of feet on the floor when walking because of foot drop), loss of muscle in the lower legs, and difficulty with balance. I am not alone. More than 2.6 million people, or 1 in 3,000, are affected worldwide.[1]

Why do I share this with you? I have experienced great physical and emotional adversity because of my condition. In my youth I enjoyed sports. I loved to play basketball, football, and tennis. Growing up in Colorado, I loved to ski. I was not always the fastest on the court, field, or slopes, but I gave it my all. In my junior year, I noticed that my feet and ankles were becoming weak. I frequently twisted my ankles, especially my right one. I had very skinny legs, my feet had very high arches, and my balance was unsteady compared to other kids. I was embarrassed by my lack of physical stature and ashamed of my condition.

To stabilize my right ankle, I had a tendon transfer surgery. The doctor took a tendon from the top of my foot and attached it to the side in an effort to limit the ankle's range of motion. After physical therapy I was back playing sports regularly, though skiing was no longer comfortable because my foot did not fit well in ski boots. While my ankle was strengthened, my condition was unchanged.

During the early days of my career, my disease progressed, and my balance became less stable. When I represented my company at a sporting event, overseeing an experiential marketing event, I lost my balance and stumbled a few times as I stood with a group of people. Someone who saw me stagger concluded that I was drunk and started rumors. It was ten in the morning, for goodness' sake! I was offended, and I was ashamed that I could not even maintain my balance without stumbling.

I could go on about CMT and its progressive nature. Today, I walk with a limp because of the tendon transfer surgery, I have a hard time walking barefoot on hard surfaces, and I am constantly aware of how I appear to others. CMT is a daily reminder of my weaknesses—physically and emotionally. I wish I did not have this challenge. There are days I do not want to be joyful.

I can relate to the apostle Paul. He struggled with an ailment and asked God three times to relieve him of it. In response, Christ said, "My grace is sufficient for you, for my power is made perfect in weakness" (2 Cor. 12:9). Paul went on to write, "Therefore I will boast all the more gladly of my weaknesses, so that the power of Christ may rest upon me. For the sake of Christ, then, I am content with weaknesses, insults, hardships, persecutions, and calamities. For when I am weak, then I am strong" (vv. 9–10).

> *My identity is not in my own strength*
> *but in being a child of God.*

For many years my condition discouraged me. I had learned to rely on my body for so many things, and I felt betrayed when I could no longer do what was once normal for me. Sometimes I even questioned God's design in my life. But over time I have learned to rejoice in my struggle because it always leads me back to Jesus. Through the power of the Holy Spirit, I can truly say, "When I am weak, I am strong." I don't blame God. When I struggle, I talk to the Lord about my resentment and shame. I don't concentrate on my circumstances; I focus on him. He is my strength, my shield, and my everything. He is the source of my hope, joy, and strength. I know he loves me and desires the very best for me.

How do I know this? Because I know that my identity is not in my own strength but in being a child of God.

My struggle forced me to identify talents, skills, and abilities other than physical ones. I developed the ability to communicate effectively through writing and speaking. I discovered that something special happens inside of me when I speak in public: I feel God's pleasure. I find great satisfaction in connecting with an audience and moving them to action.

In the midst of my struggle, God has also blessed me—way beyond what I deserve. My life is overflowing, and I am so blessed with a wonderful wife, kids, extended family, friends, and career. Instead of letting my hardships define me or take all my attention, I have cultivated an attitude of gratitude that swells up to thankfulness and praise. The God of the universe loves me, and he is working in me. He has made all the difference.

What a joy!

What about you? Are you experiencing God's joy and living an abundant life in the midst of your adversity? If not, what's holding you back?

SATISFYING OUR FOUR BASE DESIRES

The history of mankind reveals a common theme: we do not want to be miserable. We try to solve our own problems so we can experience happiness and pleasures. This pursuit is sometimes called "the quest for the quiet heart."[2] We seek happiness in money, sex, drugs, power, fame, alcohol, parties, popularity, and physical appearance. We indulge ourselves to alleviate our worries, leading to a temporary state of happiness.

But such pleasures are only short-term. They do not provide lasting satisfaction or fill us with anything other than disappointment and the desire for more. The human race has always pursued happiness but has seldom been able to find it. We exhaust all our time and resources, but we cannot find happiness, fulfillment, and satisfaction on our own.

If we are honest with ourselves, most of us have bought into the lie that happiness and joy are the same thing, and we believe that true happiness is to be found in satisfying what I call our four base desires.

- *Desire to acquire.* Our desire to acquire money and material possessions is insatiable. Ecclesiastes 5:10 says, "He who loves money will not be satisfied with money, nor he who loves wealth with his income; this also is vanity." The feeling that we will be happy once we have that new house, car, phone, vacation, TV, or kitchen remodel does not go away when we acquire our "dream" purchase. There is always something newer and shinier to pursue.

- *Desire to be admired.* We crave popularity, recognition, or being held in high esteem for our accomplishments. We desire to impress others and achieve greater influence. However, admiration has no lasting impact and does not provide real joy because we are glorifying ourselves rather than God. If our sense of self-worth is based on other people's opinions, we will always try to do more and be more to measure up to their expectations. Matthew 6:1 says, "Beware of practicing your righteousness before other people in order to be seen by them, for then you will have no reward from your Father who is in heaven."

- *Desire for power.* The ability to impose our will on others consumes us. We crave power. Without God's leading and wisdom, power leads to corruption, exploitation, and oppression. Proverbs 28:16 says, "A ruler who lacks understanding is a cruel oppressor, but he who hates unjust gain will prolong his days." Jesus showed us true power and kingship through his sacrifice and generosity. If we think power will bring ultimate happiness, we start redefining right and wrong so we can maintain power even at the expense of others' well-being, freedom, and livelihood.

- *Desire for pleasure.* Lastly, we have an obsession with the idea that happiness or pleasure is the ultimate goal in life. We indulge in a myriad of hedonistic practices including sex, drugs, and drinking. We suppose these pursuits bring fulfillment. King Solomon, who had everything, records his thoughts in Ecclesiastes 2:1–2: "I said to myself, 'Let's go for it—experiment with pleasure, have a good time!' But there was nothing to it, nothing but smoke. What do I think of the fun-filled life? Insane! Inane! My verdict on the pursuit of happiness? Who needs it?" (MSG).

The Bible specifically warns that seeking pleasure is futile and does not lead to peace, happiness, or satisfaction. Self-indulgence distracts and robs us of our potential to live joyfully. The pleasure path can lead to a downward spiral of addiction and enslave us (Titus 3:3). Robert Dean explains, "On the outside, it may look like we are living the time of our lives but on the inside, we are dead (1 Tim. 5:6)."[3] Even if someone gains the whole world at the expense of their soul, what profit is it (Matt. 16:26)?

The "quest for the quiet heart" can end because you have access to the greatest truth in life: God is the only source of true and everlasting joy.

Often all these desires war in our hearts at the same time. In my struggle with CMT, I fought the desire to be admired. When people saw me as weak (or thought I was drunk in the middle of the day!), I felt that I could not be happy because I was not being admired the way I wanted to be. Or when I could no longer play the sports I had enjoyed, I was unhappy that I could not pursue the exhilaration of those activities. I felt a lack of power that threatened my sense of self-sufficiency.

Dominating on the slopes or being admired by others will never satisfy us ultimately. Famous mathematician Blaise Pascal is credited with the phrase, "There is a God-shaped vacuum in the heart of every man which cannot be filled by any created thing, but only by God the Creator, made known through Jesus Christ."[4]

We try to fill that vacuum with anything but him.

WHERE JOY CAN BE FOUND

The Christian life stands opposite the world's pursuit of happiness and pleasure. When you surrender your life to Jesus and accept him as Lord and Savior, Jesus enters your life and begins a tremendous change. Not only does God forgive your sins and rescue you from eternity without him, he also fills you with a fresh and different outlook on life. You have access to a deep, unspeakable sense of well-being filled with love, peace, and hope. The "quest for the quiet heart" can end because you have access to the greatest truth in life: God is the only source of true and everlasting joy. Because Jesus lives in and through you, the pursuit of what the world considers happiness is no longer obligatory. Jesus offers a full life, he is extremely generous, and he works the very best for a believer.

Joy is the delight that results from being in right relationship with God. Not self-fabricated, joy is a well-being deep within one's soul given by God.[5] This well-being goes beyond mere happiness and produces a peaceful life regardless of circumstances. Nonbelievers take note of Christians full of joy. God wants us to experience a life full of joy in our walk with him.

Because the greatest joy in life is knowing God, joy defines and distinguishes the Christian who is actively pursuing the knowledge and love of God. I have seen this joy revealed in myself and others in six distinct ways: abundance, abidance, acceptance, appreciation, acquiescence, and adversity.

Abundance

Jesus says that he came to bring not only life but abundant life (John 10:10). Abundance means full and overflowing—living a life with the advantage of knowing Jesus personally. *Life* versus *abundant life* is the difference between surviving and thriving. If we just make it through a situation, we are merely surviving. When we experience God's love, have hope, rest in his peace, and are filled with joy in the midst of the same circumstance, we are thriving. Who wouldn't aim to live a joyful and abundant life?

The abundant love, hope, and purpose that fellowship with God produces also overflows to others. When you give your life to Jesus and the Holy Spirit takes up residence inside you, the compulsion to seek and strive after hollow, short-term earthly pleasure ends. The old life of sin is exchanged for God's grace through Jesus. Because of the Lord and his promises, you are enabled to live life with bold hope. Jesus says you will never thirst again when you entrust your life to him. When you taste and see that the Lord is good, you begin to learn that nothing else will satisfy your soul. God wants you to experience an incomparable sense of well-being, and that will only happen when you are consumed with him. The change he makes in your life cannot help but overflow and impact those around you. He has given you a great gift—abundant life!

A word of caution: Our enemy's purpose is to "steal and kill and destroy" our joy in Christ (John 10:10). Jesus came to give you abundant life, but if you do not walk with Jesus, Satan will distract you and drag you back to the world's pursuit of happiness. Remaining in Christ every moment, surrendering your life to him, and obeying him out of love are essential to an abundant, joyful Christian life.

There are practical steps for living an abundant life.

- *Practice mindfulness.* God has provided many blessings in your life. Slow down and pay attention to the relationships, opportunities, and work you experience every day. God did not have to make a world with sunshine, coffee, or friendship—and yet he did. Stop and think about how your salvation in Christ, his continued presence, and his power in your life affect you right now.
- *Practice contentment.* The abundant life does not mean having the latest luxury vehicle, largest house, or biggest bank account. It is not about what you don't have; it is about what you do have. Establish a reasonable standard of living. Be satisfied with your lot in life and enjoy what you have.
- *Practice optimism.* Intentionally look on the brighter side of things. See the opportunity in every challenge. Surround yourself with positive people who energize you and do not drain you. Acknowledge what you can and cannot control. End your day thinking about what went well. You will discover that positive reflection will help you sleep better and awake more ready to take on the day.

Abidance

By the power of the Holy Spirit, we can stay connected to Jesus through obedience and bear spiritual fruit. Jesus says, "I am the vine; you are the branches. Whoever abides in me and I in him, he it is that bears much fruit, for apart from me you can do nothing" (John 15:5). We must be connected to Jesus similar to the way a branch is connected to a vine. A broken branch detached from a vine is dead. It has no life. The branch did not receive the critical nutrients required to survive. It lost its source of life.

Think about a branch connected to the vine. It has healthy green leaves, strength, and fruit. In the same way, great joy is found in being connected to Christ because he is the source of life and enables you to bear spiritual fruit, including love, *joy*, peace, patience, kindness, goodness, faithfulness, gentleness, and self-control (Gal. 5:22–23).

> *Boundless joy comes from knowing that God loves us and that when we receive Christ into our lives, he accepts us into his family and makes us more like himself daily.*

To abide in Christ is to live wholeheartedly for him. We show our love for Christ by obeying him through the power of the Holy Spirit, yielding our lives, and surrendering our agendas to him.

How do you practically do this? Think about it in terms of your calendar: daily, weekly, monthly, and yearly.

- *Daily.* Connect with God during your daily quiet time. Consider praying or reciting a Scripture verse during your daily transitions. For example, I recite my life verse before I get out of bed every morning or lift a prayer before meetings to seek God's wisdom and guidance.
- *Weekly.* Attend your local church on a regular basis. Even better, serve at your local church. Connect with other Christians who are growing in their faith. Attend a weekday Bible study. I have met with the same group of men on Friday mornings at six thirty for the past eight years. We pray for each other, and someone leads a short lesson or devotional.
- *Monthly.* Take a day each month to get away and connect with God. Pray, journal, and meditate on his Word. Seek divine input

into decisions or problems you face. You will find that the time is inspiring and renewing. And you will go back to work recharged and with a fresh perspective.

- *Yearly.* Take time to reflect on your life and all that God has done over the past year. My family gets together every year to ponder several kinds of questions:

  » *Year-end goal review.* What were your three objectives last year?
  » *Year-end accomplishments.* Did you meet your objectives? Why or why not? Are there other achievements outside of your original objectives you would like to recognize? What made you the proudest? How did you see God working?
  » *Year-end learnings.* What challenges, adversity, or failure did you encounter? What did you learn? How will you apply the learning? How will it change you and how you approach the future? How is God developing Christlike character in you?
  » *Next-year goals.* What are three objectives you would like to achieve? Why is it important to you to make these goals? When will you start? Who will hold you accountable? How will you seek God's will and guidance before, during, and after working toward your goals?

Acceptance

Boundless joy comes from knowing that God loves us and that when we receive Christ into our lives, he accepts us into his family and makes us more like himself daily. The great news is that we are adopted children of God, heirs to everything he is and has. The Bible says, "And because you are sons, God has sent the Spirit of his Son into our hearts, crying, 'Abba! Father!' So you are no longer a slave, but a son, and if a son, then an heir through God" (Gal. 4:6–7).

God cares for us and is a loving Father. We can trust him and communicate with him through prayer. He is our "daddy," meaning we can have intimate fellowship with him. Part of being a child of God is the imparted desire to be like him—the aspiration to take after our heavenly Father, comparable to the way a child hopes to be similar to their daddy.

We are empowered by the Holy Spirit to express and live out the longing to model ourselves after God. Importantly, the resemblance and desire are not self-manufactured.

While God accepts you, do not fall into the lie that "I'm good now; I've been accepted through Christ and I don't need to grow. I can do whatever I want because God accepts me just the way I am." This attitude leads to apathy. Actually, God loves you so much that he will not let you stay the way you are. The Holy Spirit will work in you to transform your character to be like Jesus, conforming you into the image of his Son. While we actively participate in our becoming like Christ, we can at the very same time rest in God's acceptance knowing that it is not our own striving or effort that ultimately transforms us.

Appreciation

An attitude and expression of gratitude for what God has done and will do in our lives results in an optimistic and positive disposition. Joy flows from authentic "gratitude to God, expressed in response to his love and mercy."[6] We should always remember what Jesus did for us and give him praise. He died on the cross for our sins. We are rescued, ransomed, and redeemed, and we have a new life and a future with God. Jesus followers will spend eternity with him. We no longer fear death because we know that he holds us closely and nothing can separate us from him. Remembering these things will generate a deep appreciation as we keep our focus on God, giving him praise and thanks.

An attitude of appreciation is a daily choice and can have a big impact on others. One of my all-time favorite authors and pastors, Chuck Swindoll, writes:

> Words can never adequately convey the incredible impact of our attitude toward life. The longer I live the more convinced I become that life is 10 percent what happens to us and 90 percent how we respond to it.
>
> I believe the single most significant decision I can make on a day-to-day basis is my choice of attitude. It is more important than my past, my education, my bankroll, my successes or

failures, fame or pain, what other people think of me or say about me, my circumstances, or my position. Attitude keeps me going or cripples my progress. It alone fuels my fire or assaults my hope. When my attitudes are right, there's no barrier too high, no valley too deep, no dream too extreme, no challenge too great for me.[7]

Genuine appreciation for God's grace and mercy creates a great attitude and cheerfulness. A life without gratitude leads to a joyless life. Thankfulness is a state of mind. Make a list of things you are grateful for today. Friends, let's make it our aim to remember what God has done in our lives, praise him in daily prayer, and be thankful. If we do, joy will overflow from our lives into others and glorify God.

Acquiescence

Acquiescence means to yield our will to someone else's, to surrender and give up our rights to another in exchange for something. We are called to surrender everything to God, including our time, talent, and resources, with a bent toward worship and service. Out of our love for Jesus and what he did for us, we exchange our lives for his. In the Bible, Paul writes, "I have been crucified with Christ and I no longer live, but Christ lives in me. The life I now live in the body, I live by faith in the Son of God, who loved me and gave himself for me" (Gal. 2:20 NIV).

It is the power of the Holy Spirit that enables us to bow our will to his. We begin to trust God with everything: our circumstances, relationships, and necessities. Self-reliance becomes God-reliance; self is exchanged for God. Identity, purpose, and peace all flow from trusting Christ. We will experience utter joy in life when we are completely devoted to Jesus, daily yielding our will and desires to him as he transforms us from the inside out. A desire to serve God and his people will grow in us as we shift our focus to helping others.

How do you bring acquiescence to your life? Invest your free time to serve at your local church or community organization rather than playing golf. Instead of buying a second home, tithe to your church to support missions. Respectfully listen to others' ideas and collaboratively determine how to solve an issue without insisting on your own way.

Adversity

No matter the circumstance, God can provide the inner strength to endure the hardships that come our way. The deep joy given by the Lord is independent of the trials or struggles that we face. Consider the words of Martyn Lloyd-Jones:

> Joy is independent of circumstances. As we have seen, it is easy to be happy when the sun is shining and everything is going well. ... But what if we lost it all—where would we be then? And when you have lost everything, the world can be cruel and cold. It does not want you. The world only wants cheerful people. When you need its help most of all, it has nothing to give you, and it turns its back upon you. The only joy worth talking about, the joy that we should surely be seeking, is the joy that is independent of circumstances.[8]

The key to facing adversity is to trust Jesus and open yourself to the ministry of the Holy Spirit. In tough moments, you can pray and tell the Lord your struggles, anguish, and pain. Realize that circumstances might not change, but the Lord will change you in the midst of them. Whatever your circumstances, taking refuge in God is the best place for you. He is in the business of transforming lives through the Holy Spirit, and he is on your side. If you lean on him, you will discover great strength to endure any challenge and experience unshakable joy.

When your circumstances are overwhelming or painful, consider reading the Psalms or the book of Job. Grief, sadness, devastation, and the seeming unfairness of life were not unknown to the authors of the Bible. Remember that God sees you, knows what you are going through, and loves you. Consider journaling about previous times in your life when God has shown himself faithful through trials, or commit to praising God for his power and sovereignty even when your own life feels out of control.

THE "OXYGEN TO THE SOUL"

In a world where negativity and criticism bombard us constantly, joy can be a rare reality. Pain and failure are regular parts of life, and these daily assaults can result in our families, coworkers, church members, and neighbors feeling exhausted, doubtful, anxious, and insecure. Discouraged, they may not be able to see a path forward.

In these moments, when we have carefully cultivated God's joy in our own lives, we can speak life into others (Prov. 18:21). Congressman George M. Adams once said encouragement is "oxygen to the soul." Encouragement provides energy and enthusiasm. It builds others up and helps them overcome adversity. Mark Twain writes, "I can live on a good compliment two weeks with nothing else to eat."[9] Positive, uplifting words make a difference.

When a discipled leader delights his or her team or individual contributors, this will in turn cause them to delight in their work and delight their customers. This is where magic moments occur, where the team exceeds expectations by going above and beyond the goal. This is where simple words of encouragement flowing from a joyful heart can alter the trajectory of a career or even a company.

When you have an opportunity for encouragement, just as I did with Craig when our defective displays were breaking down, I challenge you to do several things:

- *Show you care.* Theodore Roosevelt once said, "Nobody cares how much you know until they know how much you care." Get to know your people—their interests, families, friends, needs, hopes, dreams, and fears. Take a genuine interest in them and make them feel valued. Your encouragement will be much more intentional and specific if you know what makes each team member tick. Help them achieve their goals and reach their potential. And always be accessible, approachable, and open to feedback.

- *Speak kind words.* Speak to the heart. Inspire followers to achieve great things or overcome insurmountable obstacles. The Bible says, "Kind words are like honey—sweet to the soul and healthy for the body" (Prov. 16:24 NLT). Liberally and frequently hand out honest, thoughtful words of affirmation to others and you will energize them.

- *Cheer them on.* Lavishly praise others when they are growing, learning, and delivering results. Especially when your employees or co-workers are experiencing challenges, encourage them to keep going. Show your support and express your approval. Help them believe in themselves.

- *Provide direction.* Encouragement should often be coupled with direction. Once you have offered encouragement, point to higher performance and creative problem-solving. Help individuals develop a plan, or provide them with specific action steps. Leverage their renewed confidence to help them see what can and needs to be done in the midst of challenging circumstances.

- *Reflect on mistakes.* Once a failure has happened, a problem is solved, or an adversity is overcome, take the time to look back, learn, and grow. Determine what caused the problem and what can be done differently in the future. Also, identify what role encouragement played in the individual's ability to rise above the difficult circumstances. When team members see not only your commitment to encouragement but also your follow-through after hardship in the workplace, they will be more likely to come to you when they face new challenges.

- *Celebrate successes.* Set high expectations. Once a person or team achieves the goal, affirm them and celebrate the accomplishment. Also, recognize small wins often because these build positive momentum. Appropriate recognition could include a handwritten note, a gift card to a favorite restaurant, a paid vacation day, tickets to a big event, or even a small bonus.

Encouraging others is a choice you make, and it flows out of a joyful heart. If you choose to lift others up and practice these principles, you will become a joyful, encouraging leader that others will want to follow.

LEADING OUT OF JOY

Craig stood in my office, visibly shaken, certain he was going to be fired because of the defective marketing displays.

I looked him straight in the eye. "No. You're not going to lose your job. This was a *mistake*. You've got all of the skills and resources necessary to solve the problem quickly."

Craig's demeanor changed.

I continued. "What's important right now is to focus on the solution, then learn from the failure. I'd rather have someone on my team who is battle-tested. I believe in you, and this will all work out in the long run."

With this encouragement, Craig broke a slight smile for the first time in two days. He said thanks and left my office.

Treat people well because someday they may forget what you said or did but will remember how you made them feel.

Then Craig helped solve the problem. We reached out to the display's supplier for additional thinking and solutions. Initially, the supplier offered a display reinforcement, but, when applied, the unit still looked below our standards. We landed on a square, tank-like design that would accommodate consumer rummaging and overfilling. The supplier shipped the new tank-like displays to replace the defective ones.

Even though it was a costly solution, it was a solution nonetheless. Craig and I both kept our jobs, and the company did not go under. Craig's ability to take ownership and to think and act quickly—sprinkled with more encouragement from me—enabled our company to reach its goals. In fact, Craig continued to grow in his role and even won a few industry awards along the way.

I love this story not just because company-wide disaster was averted and Craig found a solution despite his distress, but because it reminds me how much *encouragement* is a lost art. Discipled leaders drive results through delighting others. Joy is a distinctively Christian character trait, and discipled leaders intentionally allow their joy to overflow into other people and their environments. Joyful leaders are inspiring, passionate, enthusiastic, affirming, encouraging, and optimistic. They delight in what they do and focus on people first, then performance and treasure, while accomplishing great things with their teams.

Leading out of joy helps you emotionally connect with others because your authentic and transparent approach is attractive to others. You will build strong relationships with people, and they will find delight in working with you. Treat people well because someday they may forget what you said or did but will remember how you made them feel.

As a disciple, choose joy. As a leader, delight others.

QUESTIONS

- When is the last time you encouraged someone? How can the principles of encouragement in this chapter help someone who has lost confidence, faced challenging circumstances, or failed at something?
- Have you ever worked with a delightful leader? What were the qualities about the person you admired most? What was his or her impact on you? What can you learn and apply from the delightful leader's approach?
- Identify three people in your life who have a positive attitude and three with negative attitudes. What do you notice about them, and what impact does it have on those around them?
- How do you deal with adversity? What's working and not working? Why?
- How will these discipleship and leadership principles help you transform your workplace through your pursuit of Christ?

CHAPTER NINE

YIELD

As a disciple, exchange your life.

As a leader, live and learn.

I have been crucified with Christ and I no longer live, but Christ lives in me. The life I now live in the body, I live by faith in the Son of God, who loved me and gave himself for me.

—GALATIANS 2:20 NIV

I DRUMMED MY fingers on my desk at work. My phone was about to ring, and I was going to have to discuss Amy's less-than-stellar performance as part of her year-end review.

I breathed a loud sigh just thinking about our last year. We had a strained relationship because of her weak performance and resistance to improve. No matter what I did or said, I could not seem to get through to her. I was not sure how I was going to get through our phone call.

In the end, it didn't matter.

I picked up the phone on the first ring. Before I even said hello, Amy was yelling in my ear. "We don't need to talk through my year-end review today. You're a jerk, and I quit!" Then she hung up.

Shocked and deflated, I put my head in my hands. *She's the second employee to quit my team in the last two months. What's going on?*

I knew I would have to tell my manager about the situation eventually, so I chose to get it over with quickly. I walked to her office and relayed what had happened.

She did not reply immediately, which gave me pause. With as much diplomacy as she could muster, my manager leveled with me. "Preston, you're a top performer."

I smiled. *Where's the "but"?*

"But your interpersonal skills leave something to be desired."

There it is. My smile evaporated.

"If you want to continue managing people and advancing in our organization, you'll need to change your leadership and communication style."

Hundreds of choice words sprang to mind, but I chose a diplomatic word: "How?"

"I don't know, Preston. Just go figure it out!"

I nodded outwardly and headed back to my office. Inwardly, every fear and self-doubt attacked me at once. *How can I be a top performer and not be a great manager? That just doesn't make sense! How can my boss be happy with what I'm doing but not the way I'm doing it? Results are results, right?*

It seemed like a longer walk back to my office than normal. And Amy's words kept echoing in my mind: *You're a jerk. You're a jerk. You're a jerk.*

The challenges you face are opportunities to learn and grow. What counts is how you respond. It is a choice.

I did not want to admit that she might be correct. But two employees quitting on me in such a short time span was probably not a coincidence. What if the problem *was* me?

LIVE AND LEARN

As painful as it is in the moment, personal and professional growth occurs when you are placed in hard, uncomfortable circumstances. You may encounter adversity, calamities, delay, denial, loss, failures, mistakes, errors, or miscalculations. That's OK. The challenges you face are opportunities to learn and grow. What counts is how you respond. It is a choice. You can become better or bitter through these experiences. You can grow or shrink back. You can turn to God—or turn from him.

Discipled leaders have a *growth mindset*—the belief that they can learn, grow, and get better through developing their talents, strengths, skills, and abilities. Having a growth mindset pays dividends:

- You will have a higher capacity to learn from your trials.
- You will be more apt to risk and learn through failure.
- You will be able to accept the ambiguity, complexity, and change that comes with leadership.
- You will be able to regroup, reassess, and move forward.

A growth mindset also drives leaders to pursue education, training, mentoring, and coaching. As I will describe later, such coaching was integral to my overcoming the adversity I faced when Amy quit.

Knowing that growth is a process and not an event, leaders make the decision every day to learn something new. They purposefully move out of their comfort zones and into the discomfort zone, where growth happens. They also recognize that every challenging situation prepares them to handle the next one and to help someone else in similar circumstances.

Growth-minded leaders live and learn. I had to endure the depths of professional despair and grow from them to become a stronger leader. You will too.

CHOOSING GROWTH AMID TRIALS

The Bible offers many examples of those who chose to grow through the challenges they faced—as well as those who gave in to their difficulties. On the apostle Paul's great missionary journeys, he had many teammates, such as Luke, Mark, Silas, Barnabas, and Demas. As they spread the gospel, they encountered numerous challenges and problems, including imprisonment. Yet, while Paul describes the team's commitment and contributions during the tough times, what he says about Demas is striking. While in prison, Paul wrote to Timothy, "Do your best to come to me soon. *For Demas, in love with this present world*, has deserted me and gone to Thessalonica" (2 Tim. 4:9–10, emphasis added). Demas was not fully committed to Christ and the team's mission. When the journey got tough, Demas left. He focused his eyes on the world and not on Jesus. He became distracted. He gave up. He deserted Paul and his team of evangelizing brothers.

It is easy to look down on Demas for his choice, but many of us have been in a similar place. At times, I have been half-hearted, distracted, and drained, and I have wanted to give up—especially when I attempt to live the Christian life through my own power and effort. Then I embraced a concept called "the exchanged life," and it has made all the difference.

THE EXCHANGED LIFE

I discovered this concept while participating in a Christian Leadership Concepts (CLC) course during the late 2000s. Simply put, the exchanged life occurs when you give up your life to Christ. You are made new. You are "born again." You who were spiritually dead are brought back to spiritual life. You are given a new heart—that is, mind, will, and emotion (Ezek. 36:26–27).

The theological term for being born again is *regeneration*. J. I. Packer explains what happens:

> The concept is of God renovating the heart, the core of a person's being, by implanting a new principle of desire, purpose, and action, a dispositional dynamic that finds expression in positive response to the gospel and its Christ. . . . In regeneration, God implants desires that were not there before: desire for God, for holiness, and for the hallowing and glorifying of God's name in this world; desire to pray, worship, love, serve, honor, and please God; desire to show love and bring benefit to others.[1]

During that CLC course, someone read Galatians 2:20: "I have been crucified with Christ and I no longer live, but Christ lives in me. The life I now live in the body, I live by faith in the Son of God, who loved me and gave himself for me" (NIV). Those words became my life verse. I recite them every morning when I wake up to remind myself of Jesus, of my identity, and that he lives in me. I realize I cannot live out the Christian life without Jesus's life in me. If I rely on my own effort, I will fail miserably. If I depend on the Holy Spirit to empower me, I will experience victory. The verse describes the great exchange when we completely surrender our lives to Christ.

But it does not stop there. The exchanged life goes much deeper than just swapping out one mode of existence for another. What is God up to?

The transformation of a caterpillar to a butterfly is the best analogy for this change. A caterpillar spends its day crawling and eating. Eventually, it finds a spot, builds a cocoon, and over time a butterfly emerges. But a caterpillar does not just hide in its covering and—presto!—emerge with new wings. No, a profound and complete change takes place. The caterpillar emits an enzyme that digests its own tissue. Then the magic happens. The liquid that is left inside the cocoon begins to create a butterfly—a complete metamorphosis! Once it breaks free from the cocoon, the butterfly takes flight, and its new purpose is to reproduce.

> *The Holy Spirit accomplishes a radical change*
> *by making you a new creation, renewing you,*
> *and giving you a new identity in him.*

As a Christian, you go through a comparable radical change. You do not become a better caterpillar. You become a totally different being! The Holy Spirit accomplishes a radical change by making you a new creation, renewing you, and giving you a new identity in him. The Bible says, "Therefore, if anyone is in Christ, he is a new creation. The old has passed away; behold, the new has come" (2 Cor. 5:17). Or as Henry and Richard Blackaby write, "We're not just improved versions of who we used to be; we're completely new creations. . . . Then, we lived by our own strength; now, almighty God is living through us. . . . We are not better people than we were before; we are *different* people than we were before!"[2]

God changes you. The Bible says, "For it is God who works in you, both to will and to work for his good pleasure" (Phil. 2:13). He gives you a new identity in Christ. Your *identity* is "who you are, the way you think about yourself, the way you are viewed by the world and the characteristics that define you"[3]—and they are all new!

LIVING OUT THE EXCHANGED LIFE

While the Christian life includes an event of *regeneration* where God makes us a new creation, God's work of re-creation in our lives is also an *ongoing process*. God has made you new, and he is making you new. The renewing process is called *sanctification*, the inner transformation that takes place as you die to self and become more like Jesus. Sanctification is a gradual changing over the course of your lifetime. God is making you holy—and that takes a lot of work. The challenge is that you will always struggle with sin because it will never be eliminated fully until you see God face-to-face.

Sanctification is like continuous improvement in the business world. Over time, you work with God to improve the quality of your Christian life by learning from your mistakes and challenges. It is like the Holy Spirit is your life coach, helping you turn your challenges and difficulties into growth opportunities. Sanctification is hard work! It takes trust, patience, and obedience. It requires living the exchanged life as God transforms your life.

Sanctification is about facing the hard truth that you just might be a jerk and need to change.

Why does God continue to change us? Because he loves us just as we are, but he also loves us so much that he will not allow us to stay like we are! God's aim is to make us like his Son, Jesus (Rom. 8:29). God is glorified as he develops our character to better reflect who he is. This reflection includes several character traits.

- *A hunger and thirst after righteousness*. The concept of *righteousness* in the Bible comes from two Hebrew words that Tim Keller translates as "treat[ing] people equitably" and "day-to-day living in which a person conducts all relationships in family and society with fairness, generosity and equity."[4] In other words, righteousness is loving our neighbors as we love ourselves (Matt. 22:39).
- *Forgiveness toward enemies*. Forgiveness is not necessarily reconciling with those who have hurt us, and it is not letting people run over us or our boundaries. Rather, forgiveness is canceling others' debts against us as God has canceled the debts we owe him (Matt. 6:14–15; 18:21–35).
- *Contentment with outward conditions and possessions*. Unlike the world, which tells us we cannot be happy unless we do and have more,

God is working inside of us to teach us that our sense of satisfaction comes from his love and delight in us (Matt. 6:31–33).

- *Habitual prayer.* While the need for prayer is most obvious in the face of a failure, tragic diagnosis, or painful argument, the Holy Spirit encourages us to pray without ceasing. A "small" problem or anxiety is a valid reason to talk with our heavenly Father, and we can thank him for blessings too (1 Thess. 5:17).
- *Freedom from worry and anxiety about the future.* God created all things and holds everything in the universe together through his wisdom and word. God wants us to trust his sovereignty, that he cares for us and provides for us so we do not need to be anxious about what the future may hold. As we learn to trust, the Holy Spirit teaches us to acknowledge our dependence on him in everything from our daily bread to our spiritual growth (Matt. 6:27; Phil 4:6).
- *Wholehearted devotion to God.* Jesus says the greatest commandment is to love God with our heart, soul, mind, and strength—our whole being. Through our sanctification, God is helping us to love him more and more with our feelings, our actions, our thoughts, and our bodies (Matt. 22:37).
- *A cheerful spirit, abounding in thanksgiving.* Jesus says that even as earthly parents know how to give their children good gifts, God in his infinite wisdom gives us good gifts. The Holy Spirit continues to show us the many blessings God has given us and inspires gratitude in us (Col. 2:7; Matt. 7:7–11).
- *A life not of depression and gloom but of triumph in Christ.* Discouragement in the face of failure is not sin, and neither is depression or other anxiety disorders. But whatever emotions or feelings we experience, the Holy Spirit longs for us to know that our ultimate triumph and security are in God, not in our feelings or perceptions (Phil. 2:18).

God sanctifies each of us in very personal ways. He does not force these character changes or override our wills. Instead, he draws us into a change process, "freeing us from sinful habits and forming in us Christlike affections, dispositions, and virtues."[5]

In addition to forming these character traits in us, God takes away our old identity as slaves to sin and gives us new identities that reflect his life in us.[6]

- *Salt and light to the world.* Just like salt brings out the flavor in food and light allows us to see in darkness, God is making us into people who bring out the flavor in life and show others how to walk toward God (Matt. 5:13–14).
- *Children of God.* God is not distant or unconcerned with our lives. We are sons and daughters of God; he is our loving Father (John 1:12; Rom. 8:14–15).
- *Christ's friends.* Jesus did not treat his disciples as servants, who do not know what their master is doing. Rather, Jesus told them everything the Father made known to him. As we come to know Jesus, we also know the Father (John 15:15).
- *Joint heirs with Christ.* Because Jesus in his resurrected body was the firstfruits of the new creation, we will inherit the new creation with him and partner with him in bringing his kingdom on earth (Rom. 8:17).
- *Temples, dwelling places of God.* God's Spirit and his life dwell in us, just as his Spirit dwelled in the tabernacle and the temple in the Old Testament and as Jesus "tabernacled" among his people on earth (John 1:14; 1 Cor. 3:16; 6:19).
- *God's workmanship, his handiwork born anew in Christ to do his work.* God describes us as his masterpieces created for good works, which through his grace he planned before the world was even created (Eph. 2:10).
- *Chosen of God, holy and dearly loved. Holy* means set apart. Just like God is completely set apart from everything he has created, he has chosen us to be set apart from the world for his purposes (Col. 3:12; 1 Thess. 1:4).
- *Free from sin and slaves to God's righteousness.* Where we were once slaves to sin, which leads to separation and death, we are now slaves to righteousness, working tirelessly to restore wholeness to all our relationships (Rom. 6:18).

The exchanged life does not guarantee that God will fix your problems, but it promises that he will use such challenges for your sanctification.

The exchanged life, with its new character traits and God-given identities, helps you deal with sin issues, marital problems, the death of a relative, a son or daughter struggling with moral issues, job loss, debilitating health issues, an unexpected career change, financial crisis, or broken business partnerships.[7] The exchanged life does not guarantee that God will fix your problems, but it promises that he will use such challenges for your sanctification and will give you the strength to be victorious despite them.

You know you are living a successful exchanged life when these character traits and identities manifest themselves more consistently in your life. You will choose more often to be confident in God, turn everything over to him, and trust him with the results. Regardless of outside pressures or circumstances, you will choose to remain connected to him and let him work. Consequently, you will experience hope and peace.

This change requires you to be God-dependent and to cooperate with him. You cannot do it on your own, nor can you passively expect God to transform you without your active participation. As J. I. Packer writes, "In sanctification, the Holy Spirit 'works in you to will and to act' according to God's purpose; what he does is prompt you to 'work out your salvation' (i.e., express it in action) by fulfilling these new desires (Phil. 2:12–13)."[8]

You will make steady progress toward holiness as you obey God.

SIX WAYS TO ACTIVELY PARTICIPATE IN SANCTIFICATION

God has done a lot of incredible things in you and for you! But what role do you play in the sanctification process? You must actively participate. The apostle Paul describes this participation:

So, here's what I want you to do, God helping you: Take your everyday, ordinary life—your sleeping, eating, going-to-work, and walking-around life—and place it before God as an offering. Embracing what God does for you is the best thing you can do for him. Don't become so well-adjusted to your culture that you fit into it without even thinking. Instead, fix your attention on God. You'll be changed from the inside out. Readily recognize what he wants from you, and quickly respond to it. Unlike the culture around you, always dragging you down to its level of immaturity, God brings the best out of you, develops well-formed maturity in you. (Rom. 12:1–2 MSG)

Your responsibility in the sanctification process is to respond continually to God. Amid life's difficulties and the challenges to your faith, turn to God and grow through them. You can do this by following six principles of active participation.

1. *Surrender your life.* Christ desires your wholehearted, unconditional, single-minded devotion to him. Jesus says, "If anyone would come after me, let him deny himself and take up his cross and follow me" (Mark 8:34). Or as Jerry Flury writes: "In order for us to know the power of Christ's resurrection, we must die with him. The problem is that most professing Christians want Easter without Calvary. . . . [Believers must] die to old habits, passions, lusts, associations with sin and worldliness. . . . We must die to self in order for His life to flow through us. . . . We must die to that which is self-centered, self-serving and self-motivated, self-gratifying in order to live life in the Spirit."[9] For the Christian, you *win* when you surrender to Christ. Surrendering is not a sign of weakness but rather one of strength. In surrender, God's power is uncorked in your life. You will experience his leading, grace, mercy, forgiveness, and love.

2. *Be a living sacrifice.* As a response for what God has done in your life, offer everything you do to him. Honor him in the ordinary. John MacArthur puts it this way: "Until you lay your life on God's altar

as a living sacrifice—until your will is dead—God's will won't be manifest in your life."[10]

3. *Transform your mind.* By praying, memorizing Scripture, and meditating on God's Word, you will become preoccupied with the Lord and direct your thoughts toward him.

I believe in the phrase "garbage in, garbage out." For example, what types of movies or TV shows do you watch? What are you listening to on the radio? How much time are you spending on social media? What internet sites do you visit? What are you reading? What is shaping your thoughts?

Much of this media fills our minds with garbage. You become what you think about. If you are putting garbage in your life, you will produce garbage. What if you focused on "good in, good out" and changed what fills your mind?

Paul writes that we should think about good things: "Finally, brothers, whatever is true, whatever is honorable, whatever is just, whatever is pure, whatever is lovely, whatever is commendable, if there is any excellence, if there is anything worthy of praise, think about these things" (Phil. 4:8). One way to fill your mind with good thoughts is to read Christian books. Some of my favorite authors include John Eldridge, Dr. Gary Chapman, C. S. Lewis, Eric Metaxas, Lee Strobel, Rick Warren, and A. W. Tozer. You can also listen to Christian music and watch faith-based movies.

4. *Be different.* If you change the way you think, your values and behavior will follow. You should not let the world give you your values. You are either being influenced by the world or influencing it. You must be different! If not, non-Christians will determine how you think, how you spend your money, and how you spend your time. You are called to be "in the world but not of it" (see John 17:14–18). This means that you do not adopt the world's views but are different because of your relationship with Jesus. Be countercultural by advocating civil discourse instead of polarizing speech. Pray for your enemies. Instead of dividing people, unify them toward a common cause. Value people and help them reach their potential. Act with integrity in all your personal and professional relationships.

Build people up instead of tearing them down. Speak up when you see something wrong. Do not conform to the world—be different!

5. *Be disciplined.* Your body is a temple of the Holy Spirit, and what you do with your body matters. As Paul writes, "Do you not know that your body is a temple of the Holy Spirit within you, whom you have from God? You are not your own, for you were bought with a price. So glorify God in your body" (1 Cor. 6:19–20). Paul directed us to be disciplined, to take control of our bodies to avoid sin, and to remain pure. We must remember, "Sin is crouching at the door. Its desire is contrary to you, but you must rule over it" (Gen. 4:7). If you do not master it, you will lose credibility in your walk with the Lord and be disqualified from being useful in his work. Paul explains, "But I discipline my body and keep it under control, lest after preaching to others I myself should be disqualified" (1 Cor. 9:27). In sports, disqualification occurs when a competing athlete breaks a game rule such as unnecessary roughness, a flagrant foul, or a false start. They may be benched, put in the penalty box, or ejected from the game. But the ineligibility does not mean they are kicked off the team. If you are disqualified from God's work, it does not mean you lose your salvation, but you will miss the opportunity to work with him to accomplish his purposes. Let's avoid disqualification, be disciplined, and ensure that we walk in a manner worthy of our calling.

6. *Be persistent.* In the face of doubts, trials, and tribulation, hang in there! Paul experienced many challenges but did not let them get him down. He writes, "We are afflicted in every way, but not crushed; perplexed, but not driven to despair; persecuted, but not forsaken; struck down, but not destroyed" (2 Cor. 4:8–9). Paul was persistent because of his perspective. He had hope and kept his focus on Jesus.

He also writes, "So we do not lose heart. Though our outer self is wasting away, our inner self is being renewed day by day. For this light momentary affliction is preparing for us an eternal weight of glory beyond all comparison, as we look not to the things that are seen but to the things that are unseen. For the things that are seen are transient, but the things that are unseen are eternal" (vv. 16–18). Amid life's difficulties, remember that God is using these challenges to sanctify you. Keep your eyes on Christ. If you do, you will experience victory.

Join God in the work he is already doing in your life.

These six steps do not sanctify you. God does. They cannot save you. Only God can do that. They do not make you a Christian. Instead, they represent your choice to join God in the work he is already doing in your life. They represent your choice to be proactive about your shortcomings so that God's work in your life is not hindered.

FIGURING IT OUT

When Amy told me I was a jerk and my manager told me to "just figure it out," I was not sure what my next steps should be. How was I supposed to evaluate and address my own shortcomings? Shouldn't my manager be managing what I was supposed to be figuring out? Why couldn't she just tell me what she wanted me to do? How could I be proactive about turning my discouragement and failure into growth opportunities?

Besides being shocked, embarrassed, frustrated, and worn out from the day's events, I was confused—a terrible feeling for a leader who likes to think he is in control of most situations and of himself.

I sat back down in my office chair and took a few deep breaths, whispering a prayer for help. I looked at the phone where this mess had begun earlier that morning, and I realized I should pick it up again—this time to make a call. I needed to call a coach.

I had known of a professional coach for a few months, and this seemed as good a time as any to reach out. I called him and told him about what had happened. I said I needed help identifying why I struggled to manage people. As I heard myself talk, I realized the irony of what I was saying: I am a manager who struggles to manage people.

Naming the problem is the first step, right?

We set a time to meet in person and discuss my problems in depth. The sessions felt like therapy, but I knew I needed them if I wanted to keep my job and grow my career. Plus, I could not stand the idea that someone—and likely at least two people—thought I was a professional jerk! I have always thought I was a pretty nice guy.

Through our sessions and my own reflection and prayer, I realized that I was, indeed, the problem. I needed to make significant changes to my approach as a leader. Over the ensuing months, I asked God to work in me and through me. I invited my coach to observe what I could not see in myself and make suggestions, even though the process was humbling. I made conscious efforts at work to improve my personal interactions. I felt like I was getting the hang of it and that my employees and coworkers were seeing a change.

After my final coaching session, I wrote this heartfelt memo to my manager about my leadership journey over the past few months:

Interoffice Memo
To: Donna T.
From: Preston P.
Subject: Coaching Recap

Background
During the past year, you observed an improvement opportunity in my interpersonal skills. They included condescending communication with direct reports, a lack of diversity appreciation, and others' perception of inauthenticity. I chose to engage in professional coaching that would help me identify and adjust the professional and personal challenges I face.

My coach and I conducted four sessions that focused on three objectives:

1. Identify triggers that cause me to deliver condescending visual, vocal, or verbal communication.
2. Understand and appreciate diverse thought.

3. Be authentic in my interpersonal communication with professional associates.

I desire to become a leader in our organization. I want to attract people, not repel them. I realize that this is a crucial ingredient in leading a team.

Learnings

Triggers. I become vulnerable to frustration and a condescending reaction when I am in four circumstances: (1) exhaustion, (2) criticism, (3) unmet expectations, (4) feeling unappreciated and undervalued. These situations create stress, and I display an opposite personality—I become very driven and humorless.

I am now cognizant of each trigger and am learning not to react immediately, to walk away from a situation before I respond. When I disengage from the situation, I mentally ask myself before delivering a thought or response, "What do I want out of my response? Where do I want to land with the other person? What will make the conversation productive versus confrontational?" Lastly, I am too direct in my communication style, and it creates defensiveness.

Application: I walk away when I identify a trigger, and I've softened my communication style.

Diversity of Thought. I can be judgmental when an idea or direction is different from mine. Arrogance drives my closed-mindedness. I went back to discover what humility means and how it plays in my interaction with people. The book *Good to Great* by Jim Collins defines a "level 5 leader" as one who cares for people rather than comparing themselves to them, focuses his professional will into the success of the company, and is personally humble. I've been a "comparison leader" all of my life and now realize that I must move to caring more for others than comparing my performance or thoughts of them.

Application: I no longer jump to the top of the "ladder of

inference"—immediate judgment. I seek different points of view and listen to others' ideas, seeking the best team solution. I no longer focus on me but others.

Authenticity. I was caught up in others' perception of me. Related to the comments above, I was more concerned about my performance and objectives. I was always worried about what upper management thought of me and that I needed to do everything I could to impress them. Excellence motivates me. But "excellence" was about how I looked to others, not how the team looked.

I also thought that a direct report's performance was a reflection of me. If the direct report didn't perform to my level of expectation, I became very direct. I focused on the performance and not the person. My focus creates a guarded interaction with others and prohibits my ability to connect with them. I can become intense.

Application: I am working to drop my guard and not be as concerned about impressing everyone. I also focus on the person first and then work to improve performance.

Conclusion
The coaching and reflection were challenging exercises for me. I've gone through long periods of doubt, anger, and frustration. However, the coaching brought me to the realization that I need to change my interaction with others and leadership style. At first, I wanted to get the coaching to enhance my career. But it ended up being so much more. My thoughts and interactions, professionally and personally, improved significantly. While I've made a bunch of changes, I still have a long way to go.

The difficult circumstances this year were the conduit to a gift, a gift of change. Thank you!

After months of soul-searching, I made specific plans to exchange my negative leadership traits for positive qualities that have since served me well, within both my professional life and my personal life. I kept my job. My manager seemed pleased with the actions I took to rectify the situation. And no one else quit on me that year—at least with the stated reason of "You're a jerk!"

The trial I experienced forced personal and behavioral changes. Good, maturing characteristics emerged in me as a result of that disastrous day. When you face similar challenges as a workplace leader, I encourage you to take action.

- *Become self-aware.* Ask God to help you become aware of your emotions, desires, and motives, and how they impact others. No one likes to see pride, selfishness, weakness, arrogance, or failure in themselves, so this process of self-reflection requires grace and patience. This will likely be difficult at first. Reflect on the challenge at hand and determine your contribution. Ask others involved in the challenge—or trusted friends and family who can offer outside perspective—how you contributed to the challenge. Listen closely; do not internally list reasons that their perspective is wrong. Do not think too highly of yourself. Keep in mind the words of the apostle Paul: "For by the grace given me I say to every one of you: Do not think of yourself more highly than you ought, but rather think of yourself with sober judgment, in accordance with the faith God has distributed to each of you" (Rom. 12:3 NIV).
- *Be coachable.* Find a mentor or professional coach who will help you define reality, assess options, and determine an improvement action plan. Be receptive to feedback and accountability. Build in time to feel frustrated and resistant to the advice. Ask for constructive criticism balanced with honest encouragement and praise. Schedule a follow-up about your improvement plan, and ask the hard questions about whether you are making progress.
- *Commit to change.* Once you are aware of how you impact others and have an action plan in place, actively participate in the change process. Create manageable, measurable goals for improvement. Extend yourself grace when you do not change as quickly as you would like. Remind yourself that your response to setbacks is more

important than the setback itself. Commit wholeheartedly to what the Lord is doing in you and through you. If you do, you will reap the benefits of the catalytic trial.

If you become self-aware, are coachable, and commit to change, you will become a mature leader. You will have lived, and you will have learned.

WHERE REAL LIFE MEETS THE EXCHANGED LIFE

What will you do when adversity comes? How will you react when the world distracts you or you are discouraged because you do not see God at work in your life? Will you be like Demas, who loved the things of this world and walked away? Or will you be like Paul and his other coworkers, who lived out the exchanged life, allowed God to grow them through the challenges, and walked victoriously regardless of the circumstances?

The exchanged life is not easy, but it is the only one worth living. My prayer and hope is that you will yield to God and trust him. If you do, your reward will be great!

As a disciple, exchange your life.

As a leader, live and learn.

QUESTIONS

- How self-aware do you think you are? How well do you learn from your experiences? How can you improve in this area?
- Do you know someone who puts others first? What are the positive qualities that you admire in the person? How can you model the individual's behavior in the future?
- Do you have a coach or mentor who can help guide you through tough circumstances? If not, who may be able to help you?
- Which of the six principles of active participation in your sanctification stuck out to you? Why?
- How will these discipleship and leadership principles help you transform your workplace through your pursuit of Christ?

CHAPTER TEN

DISCIPLE

As a disciple, make other disciples.

As a leader, change your world.

Jesus came and told his disciples, "I have been given all authority in heaven and on earth. Therefore, go and make disciples of all the nations, baptizing them in the name of the Father and the Son and the Holy Spirit. Teach these new disciples to obey all the commands I have given you. And be sure of this: I am with you always, even to the end of the age."

—MATTHEW 28:18–20 NLT

YOUR ULTIMATE GOAL as a discipled leader is to make other disciples and change your world in the process. You have been "greatly commissioned" by God to this end, and in your role as a leader, he has given you influence over others for this reason. It is up to you to make the best use of your influence, and it is up to God to change people's lives.

I once chaperoned a group of high schoolers on a mission trip to Lima, Peru. While there, I met a lady named Odi sitting on a park bench. She had just heard a gospel presentation. Through my translator, Casey, I asked her, "Do you have any questions about what you just heard?"

Odi replied, "Where is the gospel in the Bible?"

Through Casey, I presented the truth to Odi. I watched her move from doubt to persuasion as Casey read the words.

I asked, "Odi, do you want to know Jesus and trust him with your life? If not, what's holding you back?"

She hesitated, then answered, "If I do, what's next?"

I loved that question. She wanted to know what happened *beyond* deciding to follow Christ.

I explained that she would be connected with a local church that would love her and teach her how to pray. She would also read the Bible and share her new faith with others. When she understood this, she said she wanted to accept Jesus as her personal Lord and Savior, and we prayed. The Holy Spirit was at work in her. She repented of her sins, put her faith in Jesus, and became a Christian.

Afterward, I told her that she had made the most important decision she would ever make. I shared Romans 10:11 with her: "As Scripture says, 'Anyone who believes in him will never be put to shame'" (NIV).

I was scared to death when I began talking to Odi, but I relied on the Holy Spirit to give me the words to speak. He used some great training I had received to help me present the gospel to Odi, ask good questions, and listen to her responses. Odi made a life-changing decision to accept Christ.

The history of Christianity is written in the lives of changed people changing others.

Are you willing to risk rejection and share your faith with someone? Why not start learning how today? Why not help make a difference in someone's life by introducing them to Jesus? The purpose of this chapter is to help you know how to do that.

The history of Christianity is written in the lives of changed people changing others. Just as Jesus says, it is our duty to share our faith. We are to go and make disciples wherever we are for as long as we live (Matt. 28:19).

BEYOND CONVERSION TO DISCIPLE-MAKING

What does happen after someone gives their life to Christ? Or, as Odi said it, "What's next?" Too many mission trips stop at conversion. How do we move beyond a culture of "deciders" to "disciples"? How do we prevent dropouts—those who make an initial commitment but leave the faith? The Bible says that many who hear the gospel and make initial commitments will fall away (Matt. 13). How do we equip and train Christians to stand on their own and not give up?

It all rests on discipleship.

A disciple is someone who denies himself, follows Jesus, learns his ways, and obeys him. A disciple is a Christian who is growing more like Christ through the spiritual disciplines of Bible reading, praying, fellowshipping, and witnessing. Jefferson Bethke elaborates, "Being a disciple means being wrapped up in a story that isn't your own. As a disciple of Jesus, you have given up all your rights and have been swept up into the grace of Jesus. The standout element of disciples is that they make disciples. We can't truly say we've been enraptured by the story of Jesus if it isn't leaking out of our bones every second we get."[1]

We do not need more service attendees; we need more disciples. It is our job to teach, train, and equip Christians to follow Christ and make more disciples. The apostle Paul writes about the gifts Jesus provided to make disciples: "He handed out gifts of apostle, prophet, evangelist, and pastor-teacher to train Christ's followers in skilled servant work, working within Christ's body, the church, until we're all moving rhythmically and easily with each other, efficient and graceful in response to God's Son, fully mature adults, fully developed within and without, fully alive like Christ" (Eph. 4:11–13 MSG). As we help others grow closer to Jesus and equip them to do God's work, those new disciples will in turn makes new disciples.

Relationships are key to disciple-making. Older men and women must invest time in the next generation, fostering relationships and passing along this great faith of ours. Without this effort, the next generation will be lost.

TRANSFORMING CULTURE THROUGH A TRANSFORMED LIFE

Discipleship is not merely about private devotion, mentoring, or your personal relationship with Jesus. Once you become a disciple, your mandate also includes influencing the culture around you. Through your transformed life, you *must* impact your world. Discipled leaders transform cultures through their own transformed lives.

Jesus describes our role in culture as that of salt and light:

> You are the salt of the earth, but if salt has lost its taste, how shall its saltiness be restored? It is no longer good for anything except to be thrown out and trampled under people's feet.

You are the light of the world. A city set on a hill cannot be hidden. Nor do people light a lamp and put it under a basket, but on a stand, and it gives light to all in the house. In the same way, let your light shine before others, so that they may see your good works and give glory to your Father who is in heaven. (Matt. 5:13–16)

To be salt means to protect and amplify God's goodness in the world and combat moral decay. To be light means to show the way like a light-house beacon, warning of danger and directing others to safe harbor. To be both means to influence your entire world. As J. I. Packer writes, "Christians are to involve themselves in all forms of lawful human activity. . . . As Christians thus fulfill their vocation, Christianity becomes a transforming cultural force."[2]

> *There is no sacred-secular divide. There is only being a disciple and leading others toward Christ and discipleship—every day.*

Can something so large and complex as a culture—even your work culture—be transformed? Yes! But it starts with you. In *How Now Shall We Live?*, Charles Colson, founder of Prison Fellowship and Breakpoint, writes of this process:

Cultures can be renewed—even those typically considered the most corrupt and intractable. But if we are to restore our world, we first have to shake off the comfortable notion that Christianity is merely a personal experience, applying only to one's private life. No man is an island, wrote the Christian poet John Donne. Yet one of the great myths of our day is that we *are* islands—that our decisions are personal and that no one has a right to tell us what to do in our private lives. We easily forget that every private decision contributes to the moral and cultural climate in which we live, rippling out in ever-widening circles—first in our personal and family lives, and then in the broader society.[3]

Discipled leaders ought to be the same people on Sunday morning as they are on Monday afternoon. There is no sacred-secular divide. There is only being a disciple and leading others toward Christ and discipleship—every day.

It is a discipled leader's job to take Christ's message to the world and, through that message and the power of the Holy Spirit, to change lives and change the culture. When you became a disciple of Christ, you became his ambassador and change agent. As Paul Tan puts it, "A Christian is a mind through which Christ thinks; a heart through which Christ loves; a voice through which Christ speaks; a hand through which Christ helps."[4] Through Christ, you can make a difference in the world.

It is not about a cause; it is about Jesus. Be bold and vocal, and stand for Jesus.

This chapter will help you understand the practicalities of disciple-making: fostering a heart for the lost, how to share the gospel, moving from a decision to a disciple, and the need for baptism.

Fostering a Heart for the Lost

Empowered by the Holy Spirit, our role is to pray for the "lost"—those who are outside the household of God but whom God desires to come home—and to proactively engage them with Christ's life-changing message.[5] The sad part is that many Christians do not have a passion for the lost. They see the lost as a distraction and remain in their "holy huddles."

Our love for people is missing, and it is often replaced with an attitude of "What's in it for me?"[6] Consequently, we leave evangelism and discipleship to our pastors. With this attitude, there will always be a shortage of those courageous enough to share the gospel and make disciples. But Jesus says, "The harvest is great, but the workers are few. So pray to the Lord who is in charge of the harvest; ask him to send more workers into his fields" (Matt. 9:37–38 NLT). Will you pray for workers?

How about you? Will *you* become a worker? It is hard work but worth every ounce of energy.

Think about the lost this way: Have you ever misplaced something of great value and searched relentlessly to find it? Like your wallet, keys, purse, wedding ring, or phone? I normally go into frantic search mode, recount my steps, and turn everything upside down until I find the missing item. I also enlist the help of others. Once I find what's been lost, I am thankful and relieved. Have you experienced the same?

Jesus told a brief story about a woman who misplaced a coin, her relentless search, and her reaction after finding it: "Imagine a woman who has ten coins and loses one. Won't she light a lamp and scour the house, looking in every nook and cranny until she finds it? And when she finds it you can be sure she'll call her friends and neighbors: 'Celebrate with me! I found my lost coin!'" (Luke 15:8–10 MSG).

The woman highly valued the coin and was willing to do whatever it took to find it. That is the same way God searches for those who do not know him. He is the "hound of heaven," as Francis Thompson titled his famous poem, relentlessly pursuing us through his Son, Jesus. He deeply loves people and wants to have a personal relationship with them. He wants to make right what is wrong and give us hope.

As Jesus's disciples, we ought to value and love the lost like God does. We must pray for a deep love, compassion, and a sense of urgency to pursue them. Join the mission and be like the woman who lost the coin. Let's go find the lost and not wait for the lost to come to us.

After finding the coin, the woman gathered her friends and celebrated. After finding a lost soul, God and heaven celebrate. Jesus says, "Count on it—that's the kind of party God's angels throw every time one lost soul turns to God" (v. 10 MSG). Let's join that mission and celebrate with God!

Once God softens your heart toward the lost, you may need some guidance on how to talk to them.

How to Share the Gospel

The challenge in proclaiming the good news of Jesus Christ is that many of us do not know how to share the gospel or are fearful of rejection if we do. But people want to hear about Jesus. Missionary George W. Peters says, "The world is far more ready to receive the gospel than Christians are to hand it out."[7] And author Samuel Dickey Gordon says, "The pathway from God to a human heart is through a human heart."[8] Because of Jesus's command, we need to overcome our fears, develop relationships, and share the gospel.

So, where do you start? So much of any conversation depends on your approach and attitude. Here are five attributes of positive evangelism I've learned in order to begin on the right foot.

Be authentic. People do not want to be manipulated into giving their lives to Christ. No one wants to be "sold" through an emotional appeal or through carefully practiced techniques. Your approach should be real and honest, motivated by love, and not about "closing the deal." When you are authentic with others, people will likely be open to what you share.

Authenticity isn't just a switch you can turn on when you want to have an important conversation about the gospel, however. Trust is built over time and in relationship. Especially with a friend or family member who is uncomfortable with Christianity, it's important to practice day-to-day authenticity to connect with them,

- *Earn the right to be heard.* Develop a relationship with them and do not view them as a goal, commodity, or project. People will care how much you know when they know how much you care.
- *Listen attentively.* Stephen Covey says, "Seek first to understand, then to be understood."[9] Ask questions, give others your full attention, and deeply process what they are saying. Let them do most of the talking. Then you will be in a great position to share your message with them.
- *Be considerate.* Be mindful of people's emotions and life situations. Meet them where they are. Treat them with dignity and respect.
- *Avoid arguments.* A strong, healthy dialogue is important, but do not allow your discussion to degenerate into an argument. Get the best out of arguments by avoiding them.
- *Maintain a good sense of humor.* Laughter is the shortest distance

between two people.[10] Do not take yourself so seriously. Lighten up. You will come across as more approachable.

Focus on disciple-making. Sharing the gospel isn't just about getting someone to make a one-time decision or say a specific prayer. It's ultimately about a life transformed by Christ and a lifelong journey of following him.

> **Evangelism and discipleship should be organic parts of our lives, our friendships, and our communities.**

In Larry Weeden's book *The Magnetic Fellowship*, he writes, "When the goal is a 'soul saved,' God's plan for making disciples is often short-circuited. . . . The biblical goal is not simply an oral confession but a life transformed and a participating member of Christ's body. Nowhere in Scripture is the word 'decision' found—yet the word *disciple* appears again and again. The corollary: Effective evangelism sees disciple-making as a process, not an event. A 'decision' is only one element of many in the goal of seeing people become disciples and responsible church members."[11] Evangelism and discipleship should be organic parts of our lives, our friendships, and our communities. We should be actively building relationships with unbelievers whom we can invest in over longer periods of time. We need to prioritize pouring into new believers and giving them the support and structure they need to flourish in the church.

Be humble. The focus in evangelism should be the potential convert, not the "witness," the one giving their personal testimony about Jesus. We often worry about how we look and whether we will know what to say. Instead, we must seek the heart of God and learn to identify with others by putting *them* first.[12] Think more of others and less about yourself when sharing the gospel.

Be confident. Share the good news in Christ's strength, not your own. You can rely on the power of the Holy Spirit to give you the right words to speak. And it is God's responsibility to open someone's heart, not yours. As Jeffrey Arnold explains, "A witness should be confident in the power of God, the effectiveness of love, even when mistakes are made, to break through barriers, and in the joy that will be his or hers when a person responds in faith. God will use your weakness as well as your strength."[13] Remember: if someone rejects the gospel, they are not rejecting you so much as they are rejecting Jesus and the truth. Trust God, believe the message, and speak up.

Show love. At the end of the day, disciple-making is all about relationships. Let genuine love and care for others motivate you and people will be more open to hearing the gospel.

If you apply these five attributes of positive evangelism, you may find yourself with an opportunity to share the gospel! Maybe your heart rate just went up at that thought. But sharing the gospel can be as straightforward as telling a story about yourself, God, and your relationship with him. Let's break down sharing your faith into a simple four-step guide.

1. Start the conversation. For years, I have struggled with how to start spiritual conversations. I have found that the best way to begin a conversation is with questions. Ask people about their life's journey. Ask them what they think about God. You may be so bold as to use Cru founder Bill Bright's question, "If you were to die today, beyond a shadow of a doubt, would you go to heaven?"

As part of that memorable mission trip to Peru, the students performed songs and skits at a local park to draw a crowd. We shared the gospel, and it was our job after the presentation to engage the crowd who gathered. The number of people who had questions and wanted to know more overwhelmed me. Through Casey, I asked different people, "If you were to die today, beyond a shadow of a doubt, would you go to heaven?" Many said yes, so I simply asked, "Why?"

The prevailing answer was, "I live a good life and try to do the right things." But the Bible says that our good works are not enough to be forgiven for our sins and enter into a relationship with God. Through asking a few simple questions, I was able to get to the heart of the matter and understand where people were spiritually.

Here are some additional questions that can help you start spiritual conversations:

- Do you ever think about the purpose of your life? Why are you here? What are you living for?
- Do you have the same kind of stuggles I do? How do you handle them? Where do you find strength in adversity?
- How do you deal with past regrets?
- Have there been times in your life when God seemed close?
- Is religion important to you? Why or why not?
- Do you pray? If so, to whom and why?
- Where are you on your spiritual journey? Where would you like to be a year from now? What's holding you back? What steps will you take to close the gap?
- What do you think happens when we die?
- Have you ever been mad or upset with God?
- In your opinion, who is Jesus?

2. Share your testimony. Your life story and how you came to know Christ is compelling. To connect with others, it is critical to build a *brief* story about when you surrendered your life to him. Think about these three times in your life to help you build your testimony: life before Christ, meeting Christ, and life after Christ.

First, what was your life like before you surrendered your life to Jesus? What emotions did you feel? Did you have meaning, purpose, or identity? Were you adrift, without hope, engaged in sin, or experiencing broken relationships? How did you see your need for Christ? As you form your story, be mindful not to brag about your sins prior to committing to Jesus. Also, avoid phrases like "born again" or "saved" because most non-Christians will not know what you mean. Be positive when mentioning other people or denominations in your story.

Next, what were the circumstances surrounding your decision to follow Jesus? Where were you? When and how did it happen? With whom did you pray? Why did you surrender your life to Christ to become your Lord and Savior?

Finally, how has your life been transformed? How is life different? Do you have a new meaning, purpose, and identity? How do you know? Are you at peace with God, yourself, and others? Point to the difference

Jesus made and is making in your life after surrendering your life to him.[14]

3. Present the truth. In a nutshell, the message in the Bible is this: God loves us, we are all sinners and separated from God, Jesus died for our sins, God's gift of forgiveness is free, and we are saved when we confess and believe that Jesus is Lord.

There are many tools to outline these simple truths, like the Navigators' bridge model, Cru's "Four Spiritual Laws," and InterVarsity Christian Fellowship's "First Steps to God." As Jeffrey Arnold notes, "These different methods present in a simple manner the process by which individuals can give their lives to Christ."[15] When I present the truth to someone, I walk them through four Bible verses.

John 3:16 says, "For God so loved the world, that he gave his only Son, that whoever believes in him should not perish but have eternal life." The key is to start with how much God loves us. I have often seen presentations that go right into the sin part without starting with God's love for us. I think this is a miss, and people need to know that God does, in fact, love them very much.

Romans 3:23 says, "For all have sinned and fall short of the glory of God." We are all sinners by birth and by choice, by disobeying God's laws. Sin causes darkness in our hearts and separates us from God. With unclean hearts, we feel guilt and shame.[16]

Romans 6:23 says, "For the wages of sin is death, but the free gift of God is eternal life in Christ Jesus our Lord." Jesus Christ came into the world and died in our place to pay the penalty owed to God for our sins. What Jesus offers is a free gift, and there is nothing we can do to earn it. The Bible also says, "For by grace you have been saved through faith. And this is not your own doing; it is the gift of God" (Eph. 2:8–9). Faith does not save you. Rather, it is Christ's work on the cross and God's declaring you righteous that saves you. When you put your faith in him, you receive God's grace and forgiveness of sins.

Lastly, Romans 10:9 says, "If you confess with your mouth that Jesus is Lord and believe in your heart that God raised him from the dead, you will be saved." This is the moment of truth—when someone repents from their sins, surrenders their life to Jesus, and decides to begin a new life in Christ. *Repentance* means "to think again," realizing that you were hostile to God, then intentionally changing your mind, will, and emotions about him. Repentance is admitting that you have been wrong and consequently surrendering your life to him. This includes your values, priorities, and attitude toward life.

By using these four verses as a road map, you can help someone understand the gospel. After starting the conversation, sharing your testimony, and presenting the truth of the gospel, you are ready for the last step.

4. Ask the person to pray to receive Christ. Ask, "Would you like to trust Jesus with your life right now?" If they say yes, ask them to pray with you. Here's a simple model to follow:

> Dear Jesus, I want to know and follow you. I believe in you, and I know that you want to have a relationship with me. Please forgive me for the wrong things I have done. I want to turn from my sins and place my trust in you. I want you to become the Lord of my life. Right now, I want to receive your free gift of salvation and eternal life. I welcome you into my heart. Thank you for loving me and for dying on the cross for me. Thank you for giving me new life. In Jesus's name, I pray, amen.[17]

When someone gives their life to the Lord, they do it through faith. Faith goes beyond mere belief. It not only means an awareness of or an assent to truth but a firm conviction. Faith "includes an element of confidence, a readiness to commit oneself to something."[18] Faith means trusting in God with your whole being.

This is one reason why some people do not respond positively to the gospel. If the full truth has been presented to them and the weight of the commitment appears too heavy, they may say no or "not right now." If the person you are sharing with says no, do not worry. You are only responsible for presenting the gospel to others. It is the Holy Spirit's responsibility to convict the person of sin and draw them to God. In John 6:44, Jesus says, "No one can come to me unless the Father who sent me draws him. And I will raise him up on the last day." Jeffrey

Arnold explains, "When we pray for the salvation of a person, we pray believing that God is not only involved working through us, he is also involved directly in the person we are praying for. God the Holy Spirit convicts people of their sin and need for God, and he slowly draws people to himself."[19]

I recommend closing your conversation by asking the person how you can pray for them. Most people will not turn down an offer for prayer. Then, pray and thank them for their willingness to discuss spiritual matters. Mention your availability for future discussions. Be sure to provide contact information if necessary.

Interestingly, studies show that a person is exposed to the gospel approximately six times prior to their commitment.[20] In the context of an ongoing relationship, trust God, do not give up, and be available. Eternity is at stake!

When repentance and faith are combined, they result in conversion. Martyn Lloyd-Jones defines *conversion* as "the first exercise of the new nature in ceasing from old forms of life and starting a new life. It is the first action of the regenerate soul in moving from something to something. The very term suggests that: conversion means a turning from one thing to another."[21]

Beware of temporary or counterfeit conversions. A temporary conversion occurs when someone makes an initial commitment but leaves the faith when life gets hard. Someone might also give up because worldly temptations such as power, money, or lust have been distractions. A counterfeit conversion happens when a life transformation takes place, but the individual does not have a personal relationship with Jesus. They credit the change to a positive attitude and doing good things. A true conversion occurs when someone repents and puts their full faith in Jesus.

Moving from a Decision to a Disciple

Once someone makes the decision to follow Christ, it doesn't end there. Shockingly, research from the Barna Group has revealed that only 20 percent of Christian adults are engaged in some type of discipleship activity like attending Sunday school, meeting with a mentor, or participating in a Bible study.[22] That means 80 percent of Christians aren't involved in any type of discipleship activity. Next time you're at your local church, look around and note that for every one hundred adults, eighty haven't been discipled—they don't know the spiritual practices of Bible study, prayer, intentional fellowship with other believers, and sharing their faith. It's astonishing once you think about it. But the good news is that the same Barna survey found that 77 percent of practicing Christians desire to grow spiritually, and 37 percent of those who rarely attend church say it's very important to grow spiritually.

Not being discipled or seeking out opportunities and resources for growing in Christ is like being born but never maturing to adulthood. Think about the impact on people's lives if that 80 percent of Christians grew in their relationship with Jesus. What would happen in our churches, communities, businesses, and schools if we increased the number of discipled Christian adults from even 20 percent to 30 percent? What may seem like a small increase has the potential to make a huge impact.

So, how do you actually make disciples? Well, if you've read this far and haven't figured out that how to become a disciple of Christ is the essence of this book, please start reading from the beginning again! But I digress. Let me summarize the main principles.

Teach them how to read the Bible. Give them a hard copy of the Bible or ask them to download the Bible App. I love the Bible App because of all the available translations and paraphrases (English Standard Version, New International Version, *The Message*, The Amplified Bible, etc.). You can read a Scripture passage in one version and compare it with another version to help gain clarity. I recommend that any new Christian begin by reading the gospel of John out of the gate. Read it with them. Let them ask questions. Discuss key concepts. Lastly, encourage them to develop the discipline of a daily quiet time.

Teach them how to pray. I've found that new Christians tend to be shy and not want to pray out loud. Help build their confidence by modeling prayer for them. Use the ACTS (adoration, confession, thanksgiving, supplication) framework. Walk them through each step and explain why each is important.

Help them connect with fellow believers. Christians need other Christians. We need community, so it's vital that a new believer be connected with a local gospel-centered church through a Bible study, youth group, Sunday school, or mentor.

Teach them how to share their story. As outlined in this chapter, help each new disciple craft their "death to life story": before they met Jesus, when they met Jesus, and after meeting Jesus.

If you follow these four basic steps of discipleship, the Holy Spirit will work in and through the disciple to develop a mature faith.

The Need for Baptism

For the new disciple, Jesus asks that one more step be taken following conversion. This step is not required for salvation, but it cements the new believer's intentions to follow Jesus. In addition to mandating that his disciples "go therefore and make disciples of all nations," Jesus also commanded that we "baptiz[e] them in the name of the Father and of the Son and of the Holy Spirit" (Matt. 28:19).

Why is baptism required of disciples?

At some point, a total heart commitment to Jesus as Savior and Lord must go public. Baptism is that public expression of conversion. It is a declaration before other believers and the world that the person being baptized intends to follow Jesus wherever he may lead. He or she is now uniting with the church, Christ's visible body. As James Montgomery Boice notes, "If we are truly converted, we will want to be identified with other converted people."[23]

The symbolism is incredible. A new disciple's submersion in water represents the death of their old self. When they rise out of the water, it represents their coming to new life. Baptism is a rite of passage for every disciple. We follow Christ's example because he was baptized (Matt. 3:13–17).

The first disciples' lives were dramatically changed through their personal relationship with Jesus. Through the power of the Holy Spirit, they radically embraced Jesus's Great Commission to make disciples of all nations and turned the world upside down.

By allowing themselves to be transformed, they changed the world.

The same can be said for how a discipled leader can change their world.

DISCIPLED LEADERSHIP IN ACTION

During one memorable all-hands-on-deck conference call, our new regional vice president had to deliver bad news to a hundred-plus remote attendees. But Robert got right to the point of the call, the first hint that I might appreciate the new guy's way of doing things.

With utmost seriousness and concern, Robert said, "Employee morale is at an all-time low, and the company's results are falling short of expectations. Our latest engagement survey revealed that our people don't trust each other, team members expect more from leadership, and they lack career opportunities. We must address these issues head-on. I'm putting together a task force to determine the root causes of our low engagement score and develop solutions to enrich our work environment. I believe if we improve our culture, we'll reverse our discouraging business results. If you'd like to help, please let me know."

I was not sure what *engagement* even meant, nor was I convinced of its correlation to business results. Still, I impulsively sent an email to Robert and volunteered to be part of the team. Why? Because I liked his straightforward approach, I was moved by his appeal, and I wanted to join him on the journey.

Also, something spoke deep within me: *This might be an opportunity to live out your faith, Preston—to influence the workplace and make a positive difference.* I had gone through a transformational process over the past few years to get me to this point, becoming a better disciple and a stronger leader. Now it was time to put into practice all that I had learned.

The next day I received a call from Robert. "Preston, thank you for offering to help us change our culture. I spoke to many people, and we all believe you're the right person to lead the engagement team. Will you join me?"

I did not hesitate. "Yes! And thank you for extending the opportunity to me. But forgive me—I don't know what *engagement* means or how to improve the work environment. And I'm not sure where to begin."

I still wonder if he thought I was naive or just ignorant. Either way, he did not let on, and he spent the next hour teaching me what I needed to know. He defined *engagement* as "the amount of discretionary effort someone is willing to expend based on his or her relationship with their direct manager." The better the manager-employee relationship, the more willing people are to go the extra mile, take pride in their organization, and make a difference—both employees *and* managers. That made sense to me, and I was on board to help our team experience this needed change.

Robert discussed examples of highly engaged companies and their correspondingly strong business results. Then he outlined his vision for making our region a great place to work, one where people trusted, liked, and appreciated each other. He finished by saying, "The work will be difficult because some folks are set in their ways. The old guard may not like what you're going to do and may resist the team's work. But I'll be your biggest supporter, and I want the team to succeed. Our business depends on it!"

I have to admit that my pride began to rear its head. *You can depend on me, Robert. I've yet to meet a challenge I feared. And while this sounds daunting, I'm sure you have the right guy.* Of course, I did not say this out loud, but I felt it. I knew I would have to prove myself.

Robert assigned a ten-person volunteer team to me, and we dug in. We conducted an exhaustive review of the engagement survey results to identify root causes. The team did not stop there. They wanted to take their discovery process a step further. The team wanted to conduct interviews and hear directly from the region's team members.

Initially no one wanted to talk for fear of retribution. After all, if they did not trust management or each other, why would they open up about not trusting management or each other? We were at an impasse. I prayed and then discussed the barrier with Robert. He immediately told the regional team that every comment shared with the engagement team would be kept confidential and anonymous.

People came forward and shared their unfiltered thoughts. Through the interviews and the engagement survey, we confirmed that the underlying problem was, indeed, distrust. Team members did not believe in each other and certainly did not trust leadership. They could not see where the organization was heading. They thought there were no career development opportunities. And they all felt undervalued.

We presented our findings to Robert's leadership team. The room was silent as we revealed our insights. The old guard even turned their backs to me during the presentation, effectively yet silently communicating their disapproval.

When we were done, Robert asked, "So, Preston, what should we do about it?"

Before I laid out our proposed solutions, I prayed, *Thank you, God, for this opportunity to change the culture at my company.*

God quickly replied, *That change began with you, Preston.*

MY TRANSFORMATION BEFORE THE TRANSFORMATION

Right after I was appointed engagement team lead, I overheard some of my peers talking. Someone sarcastically questioned, "I wonder who will show up? The old Preston or the new Preston?"

That question sticks with me to this day.

What did they mean? I once had the reputation for producing results, but I was a jerk, hard to work with. As I have talked about throughout this book, I wanted to succeed and look good in others' eyes, no matter the collateral damage I might cause along the way. I made some bad, self-serving decisions, relied on myself, rarely considered putting others first, was guarded and cynical, thought I could weather storms of change and adversity on my own, had little self-control and would say whatever was on my mind, suffered from constant negative self-talk and fears, and continually found something wrong in others. I was always on the defense.

But God.

He got ahold of me. He began showing me that I needed to be a whole person—my faith and who I was in Christ needed to be the same both at home and at work. There was an incongruence between how I treated my family and other Christians and how I treated almost everyone else. God put me through the wringer. He broke me through a long series of circumstances, and eventually I surrendered. I asked him to help me, change me, work in me and through me, shape me, and mold me into who he wanted me to be. What I was doing was not working. I needed him.

Then God.

I leaned into his Word, prayer, and serving others. God blessed me with many mentors who helped pull out my potential. Slowly, ever so slowly, God began changing me on the inside. He transformed the way I saw others and my circumstances. Through his rehabilitation process, I learned to make wise, sound decisions, rely on God, and put others first. I dropped my guard and was transparent, vulnerable. I collaborated with others rather than trying to do everything myself. I learned to trust God in challenging circumstances. I exercised self-control and restraint, not always speaking my mind. My private thought life moved from being dominated by negative thoughts to more positive ones. I faced my fears through my faith in God.

God's shaping and molding—his sanctifying—changed me into someone who was usable. And I was. I began building trust and establishing credibility with my teammates and managers. I had done more than turn over a new leaf: God had changed me from the inside out. Others could see the change. So, when I had the opportunity to lead the engagement team, I confidently said yes—it would be the "new Preston" leading the team.

I was ready to transform the work culture.

CHANGE AGENT

The leadership team awaited my recommendations for addressing the lack of engagement in our region.

I paused, then spoke passionately: "First, I believe people don't trust each other because they don't know each other. We need to help the team connect on a professional and personal level. Next, let's help people develop job-related skills and explore career options. Lastly, I believe we need to develop a vision, enlist the team to buy into it, and recognize their wins."

Robert turned to his leadership team and asked for their input. Some were appalled and shocked at the results. Others were disappointed by our insights. They had no idea that the team and work environment were so dysfunctional. But all agreed that change needed to take place. Robert asked for the leadership team's support and endorsed the engagement team's recommendations.

With leadership's commitment, the engagement team began developing a strategy to turn things around. We implemented a plan to help people connect and build trust. Our regional meetings were centered on team-building activities to break down silos and help people better relate to one another. Leaders conducted town hall listening sessions and one-on-one discussions to seek feedback. We developed a monthly employee profile highlighting someone's career path and revealing a personal story to connect with other team members.

By transforming ourselves,
we had transformed our workplace.

Notably, regional leadership developed a vision statement to articulate the team's purpose. We held monthly career development workshops to help people understand different job opportunities. Lastly, we developed an annual award called "Live the Values," where the regional leadership team recognized employees who had emulated the company's values.

All the plan elements were brought to life, and we got our game back. People began to trust each other, the team gained confidence in leadership, and everyone collaborated more effectively. The team bought into the vision and developed their skills. Everyone felt more appreciated. Some team members were even promoted.

We were successful in making our regional team and environment a super place to work. How do I know? Because our team came together, and our business results exceeded our plans. A follow-up engagement survey revealed that we had raised our engagement score by six points, a statistically significant amount. Our region outperformed the total company score, and we were recognized for the gratifying accomplishment.

By transforming ourselves, we had transformed our workplace.

Our external results happened because of an internal change. Each person had to choose to get with the program, to trust each other, and to trust management. Once they witnessed the results, both within their teams and within our organization, they wanted more of the same. They wanted to maintain—even surpass—our surprising numbers. They each wanted to be singularly better so we could be collectively great.

By coaching our employees or *discipling* them in the ways of our company, we multiplied the vision of what our division wanted to accomplish. As management began to trust the team with more responsibilities and team members began to trust each other, our main problem of distrust dissipated.

Looking back from our previously woeful state to where we ultimately found ourselves, I saw how the modeled change of one leader—the new capability to build trust, establish credibility with others, listen, and positively influence circumstances—could trickle down into a team, then flow out from each person until the group became a cohesive, functioning, successful team. I experienced how transformed lives transform cultures.

God threw a rock into my pond—breaking and reshaping me—and its ripples affected everyone around me. Our team's cultural improvements and related actions spilled over into our customer, bottler, and community relationships. Trust grew, comradery multiplied, and strong results followed. I cannot take credit for the change—I was just the willing pond where it happened.

I had a desire to make a difference in my workplace. To do something of significance. I wanted my teammates to feel valued and respected. I wanted to establish a fair and just work environment. To build trust and create positive change. And I sought to apply my spiritual values and guiding principles in the workplace. This experience gave me the stage to act out my faith in a way I had not done before. I had the opportunity to participate actively with God to help heal a sickly work culture. And

I believe I never would have experienced that change had I not decided long before to follow Christ no matter the cost.

There are several things you can do to make a ripple effect in the workplace and drive positive change.

- *Develop a significance mindset.* A "significance mindset" means moving beyond focusing on success to things that have lasting, eternal impact. Shift away from a self-focus to an others-focus, from using your time, talents, and resources for your own good to using them for the good of others. Rather than adding value to yourself, add value to others. Transition from spending time on things that do not matter to investing time in things with meaning and purpose.
- *Build trust.* Trust is the bedrock of every healthy relationship, whether personal or professional. With it, you can achieve great things with others. Without it, you will go nowhere. Building trust requires several things of you:

  » *Be real.* Let others know who you are, your values, and what you stand for. Share your dreams, passions, desires, goals, experiences, successes, and failures. Risk vulnerability with others and they will reciprocate.
  » *Establish credibility.* Be who you say you are. Do what you say you will do. Practice what you preach. Keep your commitments. Follow through. Earn respect by helping others solve problems, setting direction, defining roles and responsibilities, prioritizing, making sound decisions, removing barriers, and placing the team's agenda ahead of your own.
  » *Enable collaboration.* Promote an environment where people feel safe, failure and learning are valued, opinions and ideas are openly shared, and folks must rely on one another. Help people reach their potential personally and as a team. Collaborate to achieve more than you dreamed possible.

- *Create waves.* It has been said, "I alone cannot change the world, but I can cast a stone across the waters to create many ripples."[24] Cast stones in the water to make a positive difference. Do you see injustice at work? Speak up. Is someone being bullied? Stick up for them. Is someone you know feeling down? Encourage them. Is someone lacking resources? Meet their need. Look for opportunities to make a positive difference in your sphere of influence and change your world. The people you help will in turn help others. Do things that matter. Help the helpless. Be a light in our often dark and chaotic world.

To see a culture change, I had to allow myself to be changed first. Leo Tolstoy writes, "Everybody thinks of changing humanity, and nobody thinks of changing himself."[25] Do not be everybody. Be a discipled leader.

As a disciple, make other disciples.

As a leader, change your world.

QUESTIONS

- Write out the Great Commission in your own words.
- Name some people you can tell about Jesus. How can you begin this conversation with them?
- You might be the best chance for many and the only chance for some ever to meet Jesus. What do you intend to do about it? When?
- How will your identity as a disciple of Christ inspire you to make a difference in today's culture? When will you start?
- How will these discipleship and leadership principles help you transform your workplace through your pursuit of Christ?

CONCLUSION

Evaluate Your Discipled Leadership

Your calling toward better leadership is a calling toward deeper discipleship.

Instead of focusing on the latest, trendiest leadership lessons, which can certainly be helpful, the real problem you may need to solve in your workplace, community, school, church, or family is *you*. For a discipled leader who desires to follow Christ in every aspect of your life, figuring out how to fix that problem demands a willingness to look within and let God have his way—in your discipleship *and* your leadership.

I hope that the stories I have shared have shed light on issues you may be struggling with at your business, with your family and friends, or within your spiritual life. And I hope that you saw how often I thought I needed to fix my leadership when what I really needed was to revert to the basics of discipleship.

Seeking after God, I was able to manage my team better, lead my family better, serve my community and church, and, most of all, be a more consistent follower of Christ. I still make mistakes in each of these areas, but when I do, I remind myself of the foundational beliefs expressed in this book. And because I knew I would need to remind myself many more times in the future, I wrote this book. The principles I have shared have served me well as essential reminders of what I ought to be doing as a discipled leader.

May they serve the same purpose for you.

WHAT A DISCIPLED LEADER DOES

1. As a disciple, invest time with God.
As a leader, seek God when making decisions.

You cannot grow as a disciple unless you spend time with God. And you will not be effective as a leader unless you allow God to speak into your leadership decisions.

2. As a disciple, love God and others with all you've got.
As a leader, give up without giving up.

When Jesus was asked what commandment was the most important, he replied, "'Love the Lord your God with all your heart and with all your soul and with all your mind and with all your strength.' The second is this: 'You shall love your neighbor as yourself.' There is no other commandment greater than these" (Mark 12:30–31). Such love means being able to sacrifice your needs—a necessary component of leadership.

3. As a disciple, take God at his word.
As a leader, cultivate God-confidence.

Assurance of your salvation is the believer's safety net. Because you know God will always catch you if you fall, you can trust his will for your life. And when you trust him with your life choices, you can trust him with your leadership decisions.

4. As a disciple, keep short accounts with God.
As a leader, be honest to the core.

Confession is the key to an ongoing and healthy relationship with God. Being honest with God naturally leads to being honest with others, even when the stakes are high and you may have something to lose by speaking the truth.

5. As a disciple, pray without ceasing.
As a leader, keep calm in the storm.
Constant conversation with God cannot help but mature your relationship with him. When you are close to God, you will be able to weather any storms that come your way.

6. As a disciple, resist the devil and he will flee.
As a leader, ask, "Is it worth it?"
Temptations abound for leaders, likely because of our visibility and influence. Everyone knows when a leader fails. In your personal life, shun and run from temptation. Giving in means you will likely give in to temptations at work as well, and the risks of doing so never outweigh the eternal rewards.

7. As a disciple, stand tall.
As a leader, overcome fear with faith.
Doing the right thing often demands an unwavering persistence and belief that you are, in fact, doing the right thing. When an adversary attacks, remember one of the Bible's most repeated phrases: "Fear not."

8. As a disciple, choose joy.
As a leader, delight others.
In a world rife with sorrow and reasons to grieve, the discipled leader can choose to be joyful, even in the midst of difficult circumstances. This does not mean pretending to be happy but rather being willing to choose the joy set before you, just as Christ endured the cross "for the joy that was set before him" (Heb. 12:2). This inner joy translates into an outer joy that seeks to delight others.

9. As a disciple, exchange your life.
As a leader, live and learn.
Yielding control may be the most challenging task for any leader. Yet as a Christian, you are called to yield control of your life to God. When you are able to relinquish control of your life to God, you will be free to be a better leader.

10. As a disciple, make other disciples.
As a leader, change your world.

Your ultimate goal as a Christian leader is to see others come to know Christ, but you must first "work out your own salvation" (Phil. 2:12). That is, you must focus on allowing God to change you before he can change your culture *through* you. From that inner transformation, others will find your words, your actions, and your leadership compelling and will want to know more about your reason for living. That is when the work of the discipled leader really begins.

<hr>

I encourage you to review these principles on a weekly basis. Use them to gauge your heart as a disciple and your focus as a leader. You may even consider writing a principle on a sticky note, placing that note somewhere conspicuous, and reminding yourself of its truth every time you look at it. God can use it to guide you toward what may need to be changed in your life and leadership.

But knowing these principles is not enough. For you to change, you must *apply* what you have learned. You have to live out what you believe—in every sphere of your life. Whether you are managing employees, serving others at your church or in your community, or leading your family, you must embody these principles.

You can tell someone all day long that you are a Christian, but your actions will always speak louder than your words. Do not just profess Christianity. Live it. By demonstrating your Christian beliefs in all that you do, you will help lead others into discipleship. That is your opportunity not just to lead but to be a discipled leader who guides others toward a life-altering encounter with Jesus.

By becoming an extraordinary Christian—a discipled leader in your home and in your work—you *will* change your world.

FACILITATOR OBJECTIVES GUIDE

THIS GUIDE IS intended for facilitators leading studies on this book in one-on-one, small group, or large audience gatherings.

Application is the key to learning. An old adage says, "Tell me and I forget. Teach me and I remember. Involve me and I learn." The most effective way I have found to involve people in their own development process is for them to apply discipleship and leadership principles in their own lives and then report what happened through personal stories. This requires participants to articulate what they have experienced and learned, allowing the storyteller to make the link between theory and practice. To learn, people must think intently about things, put them into practice, and gain experience. They must be willing to fail. If they are not, discipleship and leadership principles will soon be forgotten.

Learning to tell an effective personal story is a process. Below I have provided guidelines for how to create and articulate personal stories that reflect the application of discipleship and leadership principles:

- *A hook.* The opening statement should gain the listeners' attention and inspire them to listen closer.
- *Word pictures.* People think in pictures, not words. When I say the word *apple*, do you see the actual word in your mind's eye or an apple? Most people see an apple. What does it look like? Use action, color, measurements, exaggeration, and other relevant descriptions to bring pictures to life.

- *Conversational tone.* Connect and relate to the listeners by conversing with them, not talking at them.
- *Interest.* Keep the listeners' attention by incorporating humor, surprise, inspiration, and enthusiasm.
- *Transparency.* Share your successes with people and they will respect you. Share your failures with them and they will love you. Be real and open.
- *Relevancy.* Ensure that the story is what others need to hear and not just one that you want to tell.
- *Brevity.* People have short attention spans. Brevity is key, but it often takes more effort for speakers to keep things short. Blaise Pascal, the mathematician and Christian philosopher, wrote in a letter, "I have been obliged to make the present too *long*, for the very reason that I had not time to make it *shorter*."[1] Be brief and be done.
- *Conflict or drama.* The best stories include a protagonist overcoming an antagonist. Everyone loves to support an underdog or someone who overcame a challenge.
- *Recency.* To gain the most from the book, practice the principle during the current week and share what you learned.
- *Structure.* Most successful stories include an opening statement, a few key points, and a conclusion. They move from point A to point B. Arrange thoughts in a from/to, past/present/future, before/after, or problem/solution structure.
- *Charge.* What are you asking the audience to do based on your personal story? What did you learn that you want to pass on to others? What is in it for them and how will it help them?

With these tips in mind, work through each chapter with the guidelines that follow. For each principle listed below, the facilitator should listen for and observe the disciple's theological understanding, principle application, and presentation style. The evaluative criteria for the principle application and presentation style remain the same from week to week, but the questions for evaluating the disciple's theological understanding are specific to each week's content.

Principle Application: Can the disciple provide a concrete example of how these principles are applied, and does their example align with God's Word?

Presentation Style: Is the disciple able to effectively articulate the theological concept and application? Is the communication structured with a brief opening, body, and charge? Is the individual enthusiastic, approachable, and confident?

Chapter 1: Seek

As a disciple, invest time with God. As a leader, seek God when making decisions.

Theology: Does the disciple believe that the Bible is God's Word, has ultimate authority, is the truth, transforms lives, and that there are no other qualifying religious writings? Does the disciple understand the role of the Holy Spirit? Does the disciple understand the reason for a daily quiet time?

Chapter 2: Love

As a disciple, love God and others with all you've got. As a leader, give up without giving up.

Theology: Does the disciple understand the biblical principles of substitution, grace, surrender, and loving God wholeheartedly? How about loving others?

Chapter 3: Believe

As a disciple, take God at his word. As a leader, cultivate God-confidence.

Theology: Does the disciple understand the biblical principle of assurance?

Chapter 4: Confess

As a disciple, keep short accounts with God. As a leader, be honest to the core.

Theology: Does the disciple understand the biblical principles of fellowship with God, the inner struggle, sin, confession, and repentance?

Chapter 5: Talk

As a disciple, pray without ceasing. As a leader, keep calm in the storm.

Theology: Does the disciple believe that prayer is a Christian's ability to communicate with God? Is the concept of glorifying God understood? Does the believer express trust in God? Does the disciple understand the role of the Holy Spirit in prayer? Is the disciple experiencing God's peace?

Chapter 6: Flee

As a disciple, resist the devil and he will flee. As a leader, ask, "Is it worth it?"
Theology: Does the disciple understand that temptation is not sin? Does the disciple understand the sources and types of sin? Does the disciple understand the "Ten Ways to Resist Temptation"? Does the disciple know that if they fail, they can confess their sins to God and trust in his grace to forgive them? Does the disciple know that they can live a victorious life by resisting sin?

Chapter 7: Stand

As a disciple, stand tall. As a leader, overcome fear with faith.
Theology: Can the disciple articulate what spiritual warfare is? Does the disciple understand the difference between fighting against "flesh and blood" versus "the rulers, authorities, powers of this dark world, and spiritual forces of evil in the heavenly realms" (see Eph. 6:12)? Does the disciple understand who our enemy is and what his agenda is? Does the disciple understand God's armor and the tactics of spiritual warfare? Can the disciple connect trusting in God and relying on him for strength with overcoming Satan?

Chapter 8: Choose

As a disciple, choose joy. As a leader, delight others.
Theology: Does the disciple understand the biblical principles of joy and the abundant life? Does the disciple understand the source of joy and its characteristics? Can the disciple distinguish between true joy, happiness, and pleasure?

Chapter 9: Yield

As a disciple, exchange your life. As a leader, live and learn.
Theology: Can the disciple articulate what the "exchanged life" means? Does the disciple understand the difference between regeneration and

sanctification? Does the disciple understand the role of the Holy Spirit and our role in sanctification? Can the disciple connect living the exchanged life to God's promises in Scripture?

Chapter 10: Disciple

As a disciple, make other disciples. As a leader, change your world.

Theology: Can the disciple articulate the Great Commission and why Jesus commanded us to make disciples? Does the disciple understand the difference between making converts and making disciples? Does the disciple understand how to present the truth? Does the disciple understand how we are salt and light to a depraved, desperate, and broken world?

NOTES

Chapter 1: Seek

1. Christina Stead, "The Magic Woman and Other Stories," in *Ocean of Story: The Uncollected Stories of Christina Stead* (New York: Viking, 1985), 530.

2. Henry Blackaby and Richard Blackaby, "God-Breathed," in *The Experience: Day by Day with God: A Devotional and Journal* (Nashville: Broadman & Holman, 1999), Logos. Emphasis added.

3. Lawrence O. Richards, *The Bible Reader's Companion* (Wheaton, IL: Victor Books, 1991), 843.

4. Richards, *Bible Reader's Companion*, 843.

5. J. I. Packer, *Knowing God* (Downers Grove, IL: InterVarsity, 1973), 56.

6. S. D. Eyre, *Drawing Close to God: The Essentials of a Dynamic Quiet Time* (Downers Grove, IL: InterVarsity, 1995).

7. Joan Didion, "Why I Write," *New York Times*, December 5, 1976, https://www.nytimes.com/1976/12/05/archives/why-i-write-why-i-write.html.

8. Warren W. Wiersbe, *Be Skillful* (Wheaton, IL: Victor Books, 1995), 14.

9. Josh McDowell, "Can I Believe the Bible?," in Joe Gibbs, ed., *Game Plan for Life: Your Personal Playbook for Success* (Carol Stream, IL: Tyndale, 2009), 44.

10. John Steinbeck, *Conversations with John Steinbeck*, ed. Thomas Fensch (Jackson: University Press of Mississippi, 1988), 43.

11. Commonly attributed to Dwight Eisenhower, though the quote was likely not original to him. See Garson O'Toole, "What Is Important Is Seldom Urgent and What Is Urgent Is Seldom

Important," Quote Investigator, accessed March 29, 2021, https://
quoteinvestigator.com/2014/05/09/urgent/.

12. Commonly attributed to Peter Drucker, but the saying likely originated with William Thomson, Lord Kelvin. See Al Bredenberg, "Who Said, 'What Gets Measured Gets Managed'?" A Thinking Person, December 2, 2012, https://athinkingperson.com/2012/12/02/who-said-what-gets-measured-gets-managed/.

13. John Calvin, quoted in Roger Ellsworth, *Opening Up James* (Leominster: Day One Publications, 2009), 91.

14. Plato, *The Apology of Socrates: As Written by His Friend and Pupil, Plato* (London: Forgotten Books, 2018), loc. 540 of 603, Kindle.

Chapter 2: Love

1. "Auschwitz-Birkenau: Living Conditions, Labor & Executions," Jewish Virtual Library, accessed March 29, 2021, https://www.jewishvirtuallibrary.org/living-conditions-labor-and-executions-at-auschwitz-birkenau.

2. David Binder, "Franciszek Gajowniczek Dead: Priest Died for Him at Auschwitz," *New York Times*, March 15, 1995, https://www.nytimes.com/1995/03/15/obituaries/franciszek-gajowniczek-dead-priest-died-for-him-at-auschwitz.html.

3. Louis Bülow, "Kolbe, the Saint from Auschwitz," Auschwitz.dk, accessed March 29, 2021, http://auschwitz.dk/Kolbe.htm. The sad irony is that the man who had first escaped was later found drowned in a camp latrine. There was no need for such retribution.

4. Bülow, "Kolbe, the Saint from Auschwitz."

5. Binder, "Franciszek Gajowniczek Dead."

6. J. I. Packer, *Concise Theology: A Guide to Historic Christian Beliefs* (Carol Stream, IL: Tyndale, 2011), 43.

7. James M. Efird, "Sin," in Paul Achtemeier, ed., *Harper's Bible Dictionary* (San Francisco: Harper & Row, 1985), 955.

8. John R. W. Stott, *The Cross of Christ*, 20th anniversary ed. (Downers Grove, IL: InterVarsity, 2006), 275.

9. Stott, *The Cross of Christ*, 274.

10. Stott, *The Cross of Christ*, 138.

11. Stott, *The Cross of Christ*, 148.

12. Stott, *The Cross of Christ*, 276.

13. Stott, *The Cross of Christ*, 183.

14. Louie Giglio, *The Air I Breathe: Worship as a Way of Life* (New York: Crown Publishing, 2017), 2.

15. Stott, *The Cross of Christ*, 275.

Chapter 3: Believe

1. Lee Krystek, "Bridge Across the Golden Gate," Museum of Unnatural Mystery, 2011, http://www.unmuseum.org/7wonders/golden gate.htm.

2. *Merriam-Webster Online*, s.v. "objective," accessed March 29, 2021, https://www.merriam-webster.com/dictionary/objective.

3. *Merriam-Webster Online*, s.v. "subjective," accessed March 29, 2021, https://www.merriam-webster.com/dictionary/objective.

4. *Merriam-Webster Online*, s.v. "assurance," accessed March 29, 2021, https://www.merriam-webster.com/dictionary/objective.

5. Lawrence O. Richards, *The Bible Reader's Companion* (Wheaton, IL: Victor Books, 1991), notes on 1 John 5:14, Logos.

6. Matthew George Easton, "Assurance," in *Easton's Bible Dictionary* (New York: Scriptura Press, 2015), 63.

7. Easton, "Assurance," 64.

8. Vince Lombardi and Vince Lombardi Jr., *What It Takes to Be #1: Vince Lombardi on Leadership* (New York: McGraw-Hill, 2001), 146.

Chapter 4: Confess

1. James M. Kouzes and Barry Z. Posner, *The Leadership Challenge: How to Make Extraordinary Things Happen in Organizations* (Hoboken, NJ: John Wiley & Sons, 2017), 76–78. Emphasis added.

2. Patrick M. Morley, *The Man in the Mirror: Solving the 24 Problems Men Face* (Grand Rapids: Zondervan, 1997), 272–73.

3. John F. MacArthur Jr., *Alone with God*, MacArthur Study Series (Wheaton, IL: Victor, 1995), 102. Emphasis added.

4. Lawrence O. Richards, *The Teacher's Commentary* (Wheaton, IL: Victor, 1987), 1049.

5. Richards, *Teacher's Commentary*, 1050.

6. Warren W. Wiersbe, *Be Obedient* (Wheaton, IL: Victor, 1991), 88.

7. Warren W. Wiersbe, *The Bible Exposition Commentary*, vol. 2 (Wheaton, IL: Victor, 1996), 507.

8. MacArthur, *Alone with God*, 105.

9. Richards, *Teacher's Commentary*, 1049.

Chapter 5: Talk

1. R. C. Sproul, *Does Prayer Change Things?* (Lake Mary, FL: Reformation Trust, 2009), 2.

2. John F. MacArthur Jr., *Alone with God*, MacArthur Study Series (Wheaton, IL: Victor, 1995), 31.

3. "Shorter Catechism," Orthodox Presbyterian Church, 2021, https://www.opc.org/sc.html.

4. J. I. Packer, *Concise Theology: A Guide to Historic Christian Beliefs* (Carol Stream, IL: Tyndale, 2011), 59.

5. C. S. Lewis, *The Weight of Glory* (New York: HarperCollins, 2009), 26.

6. Warren W. Wiersbe, *Prayer: Basic Training* (Wheaton, IL: Tyndale, 1988), 27.

7. Wiersbe, *Prayer*, 11–12.

8. R. C. Sproul, "A Simple Acrostic for Prayer: A.C.T.S.," Ligonier Ministries, June 25, 2018, https://www.ligonier.org/blog/simple-acrostic-prayer/.

9. Ian S. McNaughton, *Opening Up Colossians and Philemon* (Leominster, UK: Day One, 2006), 25.

10. MacArthur, *Alone with God*, 24.

11. MacArthur, *Alone with God*, 128.

12. MacArthur, *Alone with God*, 134.

13. Sproul, *Does Prayer Change Things?*, 41.

14. MacArthur, *Alone with God*, 29.

15. Sproul, *Does Prayer Change Things?*, 35.

16. Sproul, *Does Prayer Change Things?*, 37.

17. Roger Ellsworth, *Opening Up Philippians* (Leominster, UK: Day One, 2004), 84.

18. Warren W. Wiersbe, *The Bible Exposition Commentary*, vol. 2 (Wheaton, IL: Victor, 1996), 98.

Chapter 6: Flee

1. Lawrence O. Richards, *The Teacher's Commentary* (Wheaton, IL: Victor, 1987), 649.

2. J. I. Packer, "Temptation," in D. R. W. Wood et al., eds., *New Bible Dictionary*, 3rd ed. (Downers Grove, IL: InterVarsity, 1996), 1162.

3. Richard Exley, "Handling Sexual Temptation" in Richard Exley, Mark Galli, and John Ortberg, *Dangers, Toils, and Snares: Resisting the Hidden Temptations of Ministry* (Sisters, OR: Multnomah, 1994), 116.

4. Matthew George Easton, "Satan," in *Easton's Bible Dictionary* (New York: Scriptura Press, 2015), 625.

5. Herschel H. Hobbs, *My Favorite Illustrations* (Nashville: Broadman, 1990), 231.

6. Dwight Moody Smith, "The World," in Paul Achtemeier, ed., *Harper's Bible Dictionary* (San Francisco: Harper & Row, 1985), 1142.

7. Oswald Chambers, "What's the Good of Temptation?," My Utmost for His Highest, accessed March 29, 2021, https://utmost .org/classic/what's-the-good-of-temptation-classic/.

8. Warren W. Wiersbe, *Be Obedient* (Wheaton, IL: Victor, 1991), 108.

9. Gene Haraldsen, "Defeating Temptation," SermonCentral, October 18, 2000, https://www.sermoncentral.com/sermons /defeating-temptation-gene-haraldsen-sermon-on-temptation -30170.

10. Packer, "Temptation," 1161.

11. Exley, "Handling Sexual Temptation," 111.

12. Thomas à Kempis, quoted in Exley, "Handling Sexual Temptation," 117.

13. Michael McKinney, "Lincoln's Lessons: Endure Unjust Criticism," *Leading Blog*, February 11, 2009, https://www.leadershipnow.com /leadingblog/2009/02/.

14. Exley, "Handling Sexual Temptation," 120.

Chapter 7: Stand

1. Guy P. Duffield and Nathaniel M. Van Cleave, *Foundations of Pentecostal Theology* (Los Angeles: LIFE Bible College, 1983), 500.

2. Martyn Lloyd-Jones, *Great Doctrines of the Bible: God the Father, God the Son; God the Holy Spirit; The Church and the Last Things* (Wheaton, IL: Crossway, 2003), 120–21.

3. J. I. Packer, *Concise Theology: A Guide to Historic Christian Beliefs* (Carol Stream, IL: Tyndale, 2011), 69.

4. John Wesley, *Sermons on Several Occasions* (Oak Harbor, WA: Logos Research Systems, Inc., 1999).

5. Wesley, *Sermons on Several Occasions.*

6. Warren W. Wiersbe, *The Bible Exposition Commentary*, vol. 2 (Wheaton, IL: Victor Books, 1996), 58.

7. Wiersbe, *Bible Exposition Commentary*, 58.

8. Matthew Poole, *Annotations upon the Holy Bible*, vol. 3 (New York: Robert Carter and Brothers, 1852), 679.

9. Wiersbe, *Bible Exposition Commentary*, 58.

10. Wiersbe, *Bible Exposition Commentary*, 58.

11. Wiersbe, *Bible Exposition Commentary*, 59.

12. Poole, *Annotations upon the Holy Bible*, 679.

13. Jennifer Read Hawthorne, "Change Your Thoughts, Change Your World," *Words to Live By* (blog), 2014, http://www.jenniferhaw thorne.com/articles/change_your_thoughts.html.

14. Hawthorne, "Change Your Thoughts."

Chapter 8: Choose

1. "Charcot-Marie-Tooth Disease Fact Sheet," National Institutes of Health, June 8, 2020, https://www.ninds.nih.gov/Disorders /Patient-Caregiver-Education/Fact-Sheets/Charcot-Marie-Tooth -Disease-Fact-Sheet.

2. Martyn Lloyd-Jones, *Authentic Christianity*, vol. 1 (Wheaton, IL: Crossway, 2000), 174–75.

3. Robert J. Dean, "Joy," in Chad Brand et al., eds., *Holman Illustrated Bible Dictionary* (Nashville: Holman Bible Publishers, 2003), Logos.

4. Paraphrase of Blaise Pascal's original quote, in William Bright, "Jesus and the Intellectual," CruPress, 2010, https://www.cru.org /content/dam/cru/legacy/2012/02/Jesus-And-The-Intellectual.pdf.

5. Dean, "Joy," Logos.

6. Martin Manser et al., eds., *Dictionary of Bible Themes: The Accessible and Comprehensive Tool for Topical Studies* (London: Martin Manser, 2009), Logos.

7. Chuck Swindoll, "The Value of a Positive Attitude," Insight for Today, November 19, 2015, https://www.insight.org/resources /daily-devotional/individual/the-value-of-a-positive-attitude.

8. Lloyd-Jones, *Authentic Christianity*, 18.

9. Mark Twain, in a letter to Gertrude Natkin, March 2, 1906, New York Library Digital Collections, https://digitalcollections.nypl .org/items/53b4cf90-7739-0132-f12c-58d385a7b928.

Chapter 9: Yield

1. J. I. Packer, *Concise Theology: A Guide to Historic Christian Beliefs* (Carol Stream, IL: Tyndale, 2011), 157, 170.

2. Henry Blackaby and Richard Blackaby, *The Experience: Day by Day with God: A Devotional and Journal* (Nashville: Broadman & Holman, 1999), chap. 23, Logos.

3. *YourDictionary*, s.v. "identity," accessed March 29, 2021, https:// www.yourdictionary.com/identity.

4. Tim Keller, "What Is Biblical Justice?," *Relevant*, August 23, 2012, https://relevantmagazine.com/god/what-biblical-justice/.

5. Packer, *Concise Theology*, 169.

6. The following identities are adapted from Dr. Hal Hadden's list of thirty-six truths from *The Exchanged Life*, vol. 1 of *Christian Leadership Concepts Manual* (Brentwood, TN: Christian Leadership Concepts, 2007), 4:3–4.

7. Hadden, *The Exchanged Life*, 3:1.

8. Packer, *Concise Theology*, 170.

9. Jerry Flury, "Crucified & Risen," SermonCentral.com, March 31, 2013, https://www.sermoncentral.com/sermons/crucified-risen -jerry-flury-sermon-on-discipleship-174827.

10. John F. MacArthur Jr., *Alone with God*, MacArthur Study Series (Wheaton, IL: Victor, 1995), 85.

Chapter 10: Disciple

1. Jefferson Bethke, quoted in Jarrid Wilson, *30 Words: A Devotional for the Rest of Us* (Bellingham, WA: Kirkdale, 2012), 57.

2. J. I. Packer, *Concise Theology: A Guide to Historic Christian Beliefs* (Carol Stream, IL: Tyndale, 2011), 236.

3. Charles Colson, *How Now Shall We Live?* (Carol Stream, IL: Tyndale, 1999), 294.

4. Paul Lee Tan, *Encyclopedia of 7700 Illustrations: Signs of the Times* (Garland, TX: Bible Communications, 1996), 336.

5. Larry Sarver, "The 3 Things Needed for Reaching the Lost," SermonCentral, August 15, 2002, https://www.sermoncentral.com /sermons/the-3-things-needed-for-reaching-the-lost-larry-sarver -sermon-on-evangelism-how-to-49316.

6. Scott Jensen, "Search for Lost Sinners," SermonCentral, November 28, 2004, https://www.sermoncentral.com/sermons/search -for-lost-sinners-scott-jensen-sermon-on-love-of-the-disciples -74226.

7. George W. Peters, quoted in Becky Pippert, "Fresh Air in Evangelism Training," Christianity Today, 1998, https://www .christianitytoday.com/pastors/leadership-books/magneticfellow ship/ldlib15-4.html.

8. Samuel Dickey Gordon, *Quiet Talks on Prayer* (Chicago: Fleming H. Revell Company, 1904), 36.

9. Stephen Covey, *The 7 Habits of Highly Effective People: Powerful Lessons in Personal Change* (New York: Free Press, 2004), 235.

10. Adapted from the Danish title of Victor Borge's autobiography, *Smilet er den korteste afstand* (Copenhagen: Gyldendal, 1997).

11. Larry Weeden, *Magnetic Fellowship: Reaching and Keeping People* (Carol Stream, IL: CTi, 1988), 113.

12. Jeffrey Arnold, *The Big Book on Small Groups*, rev. ed. (Downers Grove, IL: InterVarsity, 2004), 210.

13. Arnold, *Big Book on Small Groups*, 210.

14. *Peru Mission Trip Training Manual* (Marietta, GA: Johnson Ferry Baptist Church, 2014).

15. Arnold, *Big Book on Small Groups*, 207.

16. *Peru Mission Trip Training Manual*.

17. *Peru Mission Trip Training Manual*.

18. Martyn Lloyd-Jones, *God the Holy Spirit* (Wheaton, IL: Crossway, 1997), 144.

19. Arnold, *Big Book on Small Groups*, 208.

20. Weeden, *Magnetic Fellowship*, 11.

21. Lloyd-Jones, *God the Holy Spirit*, 117–18.

22. "New Research on the State of Discipleship," Barna Group, December 1, 2015, https://www.barna.com/research/new-research-on-the-state-of-discipleship/.

23. James Montgomery Boice, *Foundations of the Christian Faith: A Comprehensive and Readable Theology* (Downers Grove, IL: InterVarsity, 1986), 653.

24. Most often attributed online to Mother Teresa, but the source is not known. "Quotes Falsely Attributed to Mother Teresa," Mother Teresa Center, July 19, 2010, https://www.motherteresa.org/08_info/Quotesf.html.

25. Leo Tolstoy, "Three Methods of Reform," *Pamphlets* (1900), Wikisource, September 23, 2018, https://en.wikisource.org/wiki/Pamphlets_(Tolstoy)/Some_Social_Remedies/Three_Methods_of_Reform.

Facilitator Objectives Guide

1. Blaise Pascal, *The Provincial Letters of Pascal*, trans. by M. Villemain (London: Seeley, Burnside, and Seeley, 1847), 330.

ABOUT THE AUTHOR

Corporate business leader Preston Poore has more than two decades of upper-level management experience, including as director of franchise leadership at The Coca-Cola Company. He has also worked for The Hershey Company, Dale Carnegie Training, Ralston Purina, and AmSouth Bank.

In addition, Preston is a minority shareholder and small-business owner of Numerica Corporation, an air, missile, and space defense company based in Fort Collins, Colorado. He serves on the board of directors and as corporate secretary.

Preston is a certified John Maxwell Team coach, speaker, and trainer.

He served on a Young Life committee, was an elder and member of Fellowship Church in Knoxville, Tennessee, was a facilitator for Christian Leadership Concepts, and serves at Passion City Church in Atlanta, Georgia. Preston holds an MBA from Samford University and a BS in management from Colorado State University.

His corporate work has been recognized through many awards such as the Dale Carnegie Sales Talk Champion award; The Hershey Company's President's Cup, a coveted national sales award that Preston has won twice; and The Coca-Cola Company's Woodruff Cup, a global top performance award.

Preston is a member of Sigma Chi Fraternity and the Sons of the American Revolution.

His wealth of hard-won experience and training in both personal and professional development inspired Preston to transfer his business leadership acumen to the Christian community. Through the *Discipled Leader* book, blog, and podcast, he seeks to increase the discipleship and leadership skills of Christians around the world. Find out more at PrestonPoore.com.

Preston and his wife, Carla, daughter, Caroline, and son, Benton, live in Atlanta, Georgia.